INTERVIEWING
FOR
JOURNALISTS

Recent reviews for *Interviewing for Journalists*

I found *Interviewing for Journalists* to be one of the best 'how to' books for writers which I've read in recent years . . . The beauty of Joan Clayton's *Interviewing for Journalists* is that it teaches you what would otherwise be deduced from bitter and painful experiences.'

Shirley Kelly, *Writers Monthly*

This has filled a real gap in the market and will be of immense use to both aspiring and many experienced journalists. It is a most practical book full of useful tips and disciplines.

Jocelyn Hay, Director, London Media Workshops

Step-by-step advice . . . her style is easy to read. She also offers useful marketing tips for the freelance.

Rodney Bennett-England, Editor,
National Council for the Training of Journalists News

Interviewing for Journalists is a sequel to *Journalism For Beginners,* also by Joan Clayton – here are a few of the reviews.

'Lecturer and journalist Joan Clayton takes the novice step-by-step through every aspect of journalism. This is a solid, sensible book . . . many beginners will find it invaluable.'

Steve Peak, *The Guardian*

'It really does deliver the goods. She takes a pragmatic approach . . . A sensible, topical work for the school library . . . in an age when young people may see the sense of going freelance.'

Stuart Hannabuss, *School Librarian*

'A compact book that covers a lot of ground . . . hard-nosed advice on the business of marketing . . . the whole book is reassuringly market-oriented . . . a good starting point for anyone wanting a career in journalism.

Adrian Turpin, *Writers' Monthly*

'An essential guide for anyone wanting to write succinct pieces that sell. Well laid out, the author gives the complete formula and takes you step-by-step through getting ideas, writing and selling as a professional newspaper reporter would do it.'

Sheila Coyle, Editor, *London Writers' Circle News*

JOAN CLAYTON

INTERVIEWING ─FOR─ JOURNALISTS

How to research and conduct interviews you can sell

PIATKUS

© Joan Clayton

First published in 1994 by
Judy Piatkus (Publishers) Limited
5 Windmill Street
London W1P 1HF

First paperback edition 1994

The moral right of the author has been asserted

*A catalogue record for this book is available
from the British Library*

ISBN 0 7499 1350 9 (hb)
ISBN 0 7499 1432 7 (pb)

Designed by Chris Warner

Typeset by Wyvern Typesetting, Bristol
Printed and bound in Great Britain by
Biddles Ltd, Guildford and King's Lynn

To all my many students who,
with their intelligent questions,
laid the foundation of this book.

Contents

What is interviewing? □ Why interview? □ Students' successes □ Learn to earn □ Types of Write-ups □ Types of interviewees – 'Ordinary' non-famous people, Specialists, Celebrities □ Overview – Sell it first, Angle, Approach, Preparation, Note-taking, Questions □ At the interview – Control, Demeanour, Nerves, Problems, Write-up □ Exercise.

Choose the person □ Ring an editor □ Contact your subject □ Preliminary research (Books) □ How to create questions □ Preliminary street research (People) □ True story □ Markets □ Exercise.

Idea □ Preliminary research (Books) □ Market □ Angle □ Listing interviewees □ Questions to ask □ Preliminary research (People) □Street level research, how you start □ Examples □ Approaching the editor □ Example of an Outline Letter □ Exercise.

Introduction

You want to write professional profiles on famous people such as film and sports stars. Or you want to expose an injustice, champion a cause, or be a war correspondent. Perhaps you'd like to run a gossip column or to report for a local newspaper, radio or TV station on news, sports events, foreign affairs, politics, high finance. All these need quotes. Interviewing skills are the key to these doors.

Readers want words out of people's mouths – the Big Name's anecdote or confession, the expert's opinion, the PERSONAL touch. It's impossible to be a journalist without interviewing skills; they are as vital as being able to write.

And these skills can be learnt. Look at Forty Questions – I'll bet the list contains some you would ask.

Interviewing for Journalists is written in simple, straightforward language and, where possible, techniques are reduced to a formula to make them easier to understand and use. But the book's scope goes further than revealing formulae for beginners. In many instances, I tell you what to actually SAY. I don't merely tell you 'make an appointment with the interviewee', 'start the interview' or 'sell it to the editor' – I tell you what words to use.

This book is for people who:

- are seriously thinking of journalism as a career;
- are regularly published freelances or staffers, but need to brush up on their interviewing techniques;
- want a paying hobby.

The advantages of getting information via a face-to-face meeting are that it's spontaneous, personal, unique, fast and TOPICAL. Topicality is meat and drink to editors, especially newspaper editors. Remember, you've still got to SELL your write-up. You must learn to earn.

With sufficient practice, in the hands of a creative journalist interviewing can become an art.

Interviewing for Journalists is a step-by-step tutorial. It's based on the courses I currently run, and have been running for some years, at various Westminster Adult Education Colleges. Most of the students who enrol are doing a follow-on from my *Journalism for Beginners* course (see my book of that title, published by Piatkus, to which this is a sequel).

This book is backed by twenty years' experience on newspapers and magazines as a journalist and editor. This is a practical, not an academic, guide.

Forty Questions Asked by Beginners

Before you get to the tutorial in this book there are, of course, already dozens of questions in your mind. You want to know: 'Will this book answer them?' Students on my courses start with the same queries.

So I went around my class on Day One of my Interviewing Course. I asked students: 'What questions are foremost in your minds?' This is what they said:

1 How do you select appropriate interviewees if you are a freelance?

Answer Freelance or staff journalist, the answer's the same. By deciding on what you need to know. The interviewee gives the answers (more in Chapters 1, 2 and 3).

For instance, for your local Potteries newspaper, you're writing a feature on the effects of the Trentham Colliery closing down which threw 1,500 men on the dole.

You sit down and do a C.Q.R. graph (see Chapter 2). Trentham Pit Closure goes in the centre of the graph and around it you write all the PEOPLE you can think of who could be affected. Do one now as an exercise. Who can you think of? – miners, miners' wives, families, management at the colliery, people who run local shops, cinemas, bookmakers, pubs, Working Men's Clubs, schools, Job Centres, police – think of all the people involved in the daily life of the town.

Then you look at each person and imagine the PROBLEMS the pit closure could cause them – the Job Centre will be overwhelmed with applicants, the police might fear a rise in crime, there'll be less money for the entertainment centres and shops, the miners' wives will have their men at home during the day, are they pleased or not pleased?

These problems are thrown up by your mind, but the solutions aren't. Neither are all the effects on each individual. This is what you want to know. So these are the people you visit to ask.

2 How do you become confident in the topic you want to ask the interviewee about?

Answer   Research. (More in Chapters 3, 4 and 5).

3 Is a lot of research necessary before the interview can be conducted?

Answer   You research until you're confident you know enough about your interviewee and his career/lifestyle (whatever is appropriate) so you can ask sensible questions and *understand* the answers (more in Chapters 3, 4 and 5).

You also need to research until you have planned out a saleable feature or profile. You can't wander away from an interview merely hoping that the write-up will just 'happen'.

If it's a feature, many professional journalists have more or less written the piece in their heads before they go into the interview. The interviewee's answers are merely to fill the gaps that couldn't be filled by book research.

4 How do you approach someone to interview them?

Answer   If they're a celebrity, through their agent; if a specialist, through their secretary; others, just look in the telephone directory. (More in Chapter 6.)

5 What do you do if they say they want money?

Answer   Money or gifts have no place in an interview. You don't pay them and they don't pay you. (More in Chapter 16.)

6 Would some people want to see the questions first?

Answer Some ask – but you should never volunteer, because you can always get better quality quotes from interviewees who haven't seen them (more in Chapter 10). Try and avoid this by telling them: 'It's not editorial policy. And by seeing the questions beforehand you'll kill all the spontaneity – I don't want measured, stolid answers.'

What the journalist wants is comments spurred by passion, hopefully, an immediate reaction. Otherwise the profile/feature could read very flat and the editor won't accept it. Suppose they say: 'But I might think of something interesting to say afterwards.' You tell them: 'That isn't unusual. All you have to do is ring me and tell me. I'd welcome that.'

On the other hand, if it's a specialist you are interviewing it's a good idea to give him a list of your questions. He will usually need time to check statements and/or accrue statistics or other data for you.

7 Is it a good idea to rehearse the interview with the person being questioned?

Answer No, you'd lose the spontaneity when you do it the second time, i.e. the 'real' time. Also, I doubt if anyone would give you two appointments, most people are too busy. But see Chapter 9 on practice interviewing.

8 How important is the venue for the interview?

Answer Very important. It's vital that you, and especially your subject, feel relaxed. (More in Chapter 7.)

If either of you are nervous about the venue – you're in somebody else's house and you're afraid they may come into the room, or one of you has to concentrate on driving the car – then there's not going to be total concentration on the questions and answers.

Another essential point is that there's no extraneous noise such as traffic, children playing, music, cutlery being used or other people talking – they could drown the words on the tape.

Additionally, it's important that there aren't any interruptions, like your interviewee's children barging in, or their spouse bringing cups of tea, or the telephone ringing. All these will be recorded on your machine and make transcription difficult, if not impossible in places.

9 How do you overcome your own nerves before the interview?

Answer   Remember that everyone is nervous, it's not just you. Take three deep breaths, then go and do it. What gives you confidence is that you have the advantage because you're in control of the interview. (More in Chapter 13.)

10   How do you put people at their ease?

Answer   Same as you do with anyone you meet – be relaxed yourself, showing by your easy manner that this isn't an 'anxiety-making' event; watch their body language and chat to them about non-essentials to start with; keep your voice down; pay them a slight compliment perhaps; smile at them; give a nod of encouragement when they make a point; look interested in what they're saying; tell them they're not as nervous as you are; tell them you've never lost an interviewee yet; ask if there's anything in particular that they're anxious about (if so, reassure them).

All this is to show them that you're a nice guy and you're not going to grill them. In fact the session is going to be an enjoyable one for both of you. (More in Chapter 13).

11   How do you reassure your interviewee that the recording machine need have no drawbacks for him?

Answer   Say: 'I promise you, nobody but me will ever hear the tape. And after I've written the piece, I'll wipe the tape if you like.' (More in Chapter 13.)

Another point: buy a small tape recorder – the best size is about 5in × 3½in × 1½in/13cm × 9cm × 4cm, then it's not too obtrusive.

Put it on the table between you saying: 'You don't mind if I use this, do you – I don't want to misquote you. After a while you'll forget it's even there.'

12 If you don't have a tape recorder what's the most effective way of writing down the answers?

Answer Shorthand or give up the idea of becoming a journalist. (More in Chapter 12.) Save up for a tape recorder/dictating machine – they're under £30 for a reliable make.

A note-taking method you can use for brief comments, is a shortened version of written words. Basically you leave out as many vowels as possible and rely on the sense of the statement to help you transcribe it (example in Chapter 12). But this method certainly can't cope with verbatim answers from an interviewee. You need to be able to transcribe the notes within an hour or two because your memory can't be relied upon to be PRECISE.

13 How do you start an interview?

Answer Shake hands, say 'Hello', looking them straight in the eye, and SMILE. (More in Chapter 13.)

14 How do you structure an interview to get the most out of it?

Answer Plan your feature/profile beforehand (more in Chapter 10). Focus first on discovering the who, what, where, when, why, how of the situation. Then ask the questions you came up with when you did your C.Q.R.

15 Do you list the questions you want answered so you can keep the interview in order? Or do you let the interviewee talk at random?

Answer A bit of both. You always take along questions you've thought out beforehand – these form the structure of the piece you're going to write afterwards (more in Chapters

10 and 11). But on listening to the answers, if s/he replies fully and satisfactorily, then go on to your next question. If s/he goes off slightly at a tangent BUT WHAT IS SAID CAN BE USED IN YOUR WRITE-UP, then let them chat on. When they've finished digressing, bring them back to your question.

16 What do you do if they only half-answer your question?

Answer Persist. Say: 'And then . . . ?' or 'Is that all that happened?' or 'That's only half the story . . .'

17 How do you lead people to talk freely about areas they would rather avoid?

Answer Experience. But if they don't want to answer, you can't MAKE them (more in Chapters 14 and 15). Honour their veto if it's about their private life. But if it's, say, an ethical matter, then you will need to be persistent. If they're cagey, try letting the subject drop, then returning to that vital question later, but using a different approach.

Example A couple of years ago I interviewed the producer of a play. One of the minor, but essential, roles in the play was that of a musician. He is accidentally shot dead in a night club. He's playing the piano, the intended victim walks past him, and the gunman is a poor shot.

Actor Ben Crozier had a passable track record in rep, and is also a pianist. He auditions for the part. But it goes to another actor who can't play the piano. The successful actor is white, Crozier is black.

My Question Mr Producer, was the night club pianist a speaking role?
Answer No.
Q Would the fact that Crozier is black have anything to do with the fact that he was turned down?
A We are an equal opportunities company. In fact we . . .

The producer goes off at a tangent and he hasn't answered the question. I let him get on with his evasive patter uninterrupted while I mentally planned another approach.

Q Yes, that's interesting. But the piano – how did you cope with the fact that the actor couldn't play it?

A Used a tape.

Q Oh, I see. Couldn't have sounded very authentic?

A Not really – well – it was all right.

Q So what stopped you hiring the actor who *could* play the piano?

A His accent was wrong for the part.

Q But you said earlier it was a non-speaking part.

A Oh – yes . . .

Q And night club musicians are black as often as not. Crozier would have been ideal.

A I don't wish to discuss this any further. If you keep carping on about it I'll leave.

I had painted him into a corner – some producers might have admitted at this stage that 'Yes, Crozier was passed over because of his colour'; but not this one.

But all is not lost. One way of dealing with this is to reproduce that part of the interview verbatim. Don't under any circumstances give any opinion – it isn't necessary. The editor, reading an exact extract cleverly fitted into the profile or feature, will come to his own conclusion. So will readers. That's good journalism.

18 What do you do if the interviewee rudely rebuffs you?

Answer Ride it – go on to the next question, because you're not there for a casual conversation, but with a positive objective (to get information). If they are really rude, get up and walk out. You don't HAVE to put up with it. (More in Chapter 16.)

But, of course, you may not be able to do your interview. A great deal depends upon WHERE in the interview you are – on how many of your questions have been answered.

19 How do you encourage the interviewee to delve into their fund of anecdotes?

Answer   After you've talked about a specific topic, say: 'You must have a good story about that' or 'Did anything unusual happen?' or 'Did anything embarrassing or amusing happen?' or 'Did anything happen that made you feel proud or frightened?' (More in Chapters 11 and 14.)

20   How do you keep control of the interview if the interviewee tends to ramble on and on, and is pretty forthright with it?

Answer   Every interviewer meets these people. As soon as they pause for breath, jump in with: 'It's a shame to interrupt you, as this is all so interesting, but I'd like to get back to my question, please. Perhaps we can return to this later.' (More in Chapter 15.) Or if that still doesn't stop them, try: 'Well that's fascinating, but it isn't what I came to find out. If I don't give my editor what he wants then the piece won't be published and I will have wasted your time.'

21   How do you cope with an interviewee who is drunk or obnoxious or upset?

Answer   Make an appointment for another interview when they're feeling better.

22   How much should one probe?

Answer   There can't be hard and fast rules – it varies from interview to interview. It depends upon whether it's a straightforward profile, say, or an exposé or a news feature.
   If you've arranged the interview to dig for vital information that the interviewee has – and he's not giving it to you – then probe. If it's a personal question and you're doing a feature or profile which doesn't HAVE to have the answer, then drop the question and go on to another one. Use your common sense. (See Chapter 14.)

23   Do you ask question after question, or do you try and make it more like a conversation?

Answer   A bit of both. (See Chapters 11 and 14.)

24   Is there anything you take note of apart from the inter-viewee's replies?

Answer   Yes, body language, tone of voice, their home envir-onment, style of dress, accent. (See why in Chapter 13.)

25   How do you deduce information that isn't being given by the interviewee and which they may want to hide?

Answer   You can't unless you afterwards ask someone else, possibly someone who knows your interviewee.

26   How do you come up with original questions if your inter-viewee is a celebrity who's been interviewed a lot?

Answer   I give you three methods. (See Chapters 2, 10 and 11).
   (a) Read as many profiles as you can – not dozens, but a hundred. Note the questions asked.
   (b) Do a C.Q.R.
   (c) Think up off-beat questions such as: 'If you weren't a film actor/novelist (whatever), what would you rather be?' or 'What talent don't you possess that you wish you had?' Either of those answers you can follow with 'Why?' which should unleash a fruitful dialogue between you.

27   How long should you interview for?

Answer   At least an hour – possibly two if it's for a profile. For a feature half an hour is probably long enough.

28   How do you make your exit from an interview?

Answer   It's courteous to let your subject know you are coming to the end. Just say: 'One last question, Mr Smith . . .' (More in Chapter 16.)

29 After the interview, which you've taped, what do you do if you can't understand some of the answer because the words aren't clear?

Answer Try and write the piece avoiding the unclear words. Get a better quality tape or tape recorder if this problem persists (more in Chapter 12). Phone the interviewee if it's imperative you use those exact words, and ask them if they can remember what they said (but this makes you look rather amateur).

30 How much of what you said at the interview can you turn into quotes in the write-up?

Answer None. You can't invent quotes. (More on this in Chapter 14.) The only instance is if you asked: 'Would you say that . . .' then you can put into quotes the words they heard you speak, and ONLY those. For example: 'Would you say the actress was aged between 26 and 36?' and they answered: 'Yes.' In your feature/profile, ethics insist that you can only write: 'Mr Dodds said the actress's age was between 26 and 36' because that, and only that, is what he agreed to at the interview.

31 How do you write up the interview in a way that's interesting and revealing?

Answer Ask the right questions in the first place so you have interesting and revealing answers. Then study/analyse profiles and features printed in newspapers and magazines and emulate their style. Come on one of my *Journalism for Beginners* courses! (Also see Chapters 19 and 20.)

32 How do I become a confident interviewer?

Answer Practise.

33 Can you interview someone on the spot or should you ask to meet them somewhere later?

Answer Either – whichever is most convenient to you both.

34 What's the best way to approach 'ordinary' people who aren't used to being interviewed?

Answer Don't say: 'I want to interview you' as this might scare them. Say: 'Could we just talk about this? Let's find somewhere to sit down comfortably' or 'Could I take you for a coffee?' This is for just a question or two only. A full-scale interview is too difficult at a meal table or in a restaurant/café. (See Chapters 2, 3 and 4.)

35 What do you do if your editor sends you to interview someone, and they drop a bombshell of news for which you just aren't prepared?

Answer This is thinking on your feet time – see Chapter 16 under 'Bombshell'.

36 Are there any legalities beginner journalists should be aware of?

Answer Yes, many. I cover many of them in Chapter 17, but your best friend is an excellent book: *McNae's Essential Law for Journalists* by Tom Welsh and Walter Greenwood, published by Butterworths.

37 How do you sell what you've written?

Answer Contact the editor of a publication that buys the type of write-up you have to sell (more in Chapters 2, 3 and 21).

38 Is journalism a very competitive industry to enter into?

Answer Yes, viciously so. The recession has resulted in many staff journalists being made redundant. Most immediately become freelances – with the advantage of EXPERIENCE.

39 Which is the easiest area to start working in: radio, TV, newsapapers, or magazines?

Answer   There isn't one. I myself favour magazines. Forget TV all together, it's more or less a closed shop. Leave national radio alone, too, but regional still takes contributions from freelances.

As for magazines – you will have to go to a big newsagent and look at them all. If they DON'T print a statement that they won't consider unsolicited work, then it's OK to submit work to them for consideration.

Don't rely on *The Writers' & Artists' Yearbook* or *The Writer's Handbook* – they're both great sources of reference but, like any yearbook the information they have on the particular magazine you're interested in could be 12 months out of date. With a recession on, publications can change their policies overnight.

As for newspapers – to begin with, your local and regional papers are more realistic targets than the nationals.

40   How do you cope with child interviewees?

Answer   Treat them like adults, just be extra kind. And if they're in shock (they could have seen their house burn down or a relative killed), don't badger them. And remember they often say things they wouldn't say in calmer moments. So respect this, (see Press Complaints Commission's Code of Practice, page 102.

EXERCISE

How many questions can you add to these forty?

If you can think up   5 – you're keen;

  "   "   "   "   " 10 – you're very keen;

  "   "   "   "   " 15 – you're extremely keen;

  "   "   "   "   " 20 – you're going to become an expert
                                              interviewer.

CHAPTER 1

Quotes are Journalism's Vitality

- What is interviewing
- Why interview?
- Students' successes
- Learn to earn
- Types of write-ups
- Types of interviewees – 'ordinary' non-famous people, specialists, celebrities
- Overview – Sell it first, Angle, Approach, Preparation, Note-taking, Questions
- At the interview – Control, Demeanour, Nerves, Problems, Write-up
- Exercise.

INTERVIEWING is a means of getting information from other people. This book is to help established and beginner journalists to get facts, opinions and anecdotes so they can write professional, vivific news stories, news features and profiles. Quotes are journalism's vitality.

Interviewing is a skill as essential to the journalist as being able to write. But it is, of course, merely a means to an end – this being the piece you submit to an editor. The quality of your final write-up depends on the quality of your interview.

A successful journalist's talent is not singularly a mastery of the written word. That represents only a quarter of their omnicompetence, which is made up like this:

- 25 per cent interviewer;
- 25 per cent investigator/researcher;
- 25 per cent salesman;
- 25 per cent writer.

The majority of professional journalists are paid for every word they write. But they don't become professionals until they've learned the most effective way of tackling all these four skills.

WHY BOTHER TO INTERVIEW?

Quotes are necessary to turn a short piece of non-fiction (an article), into a piece of journalism. You can't get quotes unless you interview people.

An ARTICLE is a short, non-fiction piece based entirely on book research with probably a bit of personal experience thrown in for authenticity.

On the other hand, FEATURES and PROFILES are journalism. They are pieces of short non-fiction that LIVE. Yes, they have book research and often personal experience. But they go much further. Their added extra is that they are vivified by the comments, opinions, and anecdotes of people other than the writer, who can only have one person's restricted outlook.

Today's newspaper and magazine readers want more than straightforward factual accounts of situations. In the first place they want to know WHY such-and-such happened – the emotions that motivated the action – and what happens now. And they want that information straight from the horse's mouth – the person involved.

It's the quotes that 'make it real', give it vitality. Readers can take only so much commentary/narrative/opinion from the writer. The excitement – that ingredient known as 'human interest' – comes mostly from quotes.

And makes it unique. My suggestions in this book are only guidelines. The really creative part is using my guidelines as a structure, and then doing your own thing.

This book tells you how to handle profiles AND features. In some instances the tips are specifically for one or the other – and I say so. If I don't, then the advice applies to both types.

STUDENTS' SUCCESSES

Every piece you work on usually needs you to interview at least one person.

Let's look at five examples. As I have already mentioned, I run 'Interviewing for Journalists' courses – upon which this book is based. These are the most recent pieces of journalism that five of my students had accepted:

(a) *The Observer* – interview with ex-director of the English National Ballet, Peter Schaufuss;
(b) *Money Mail* in the *Daily Mail* – an interview with a solicitor on legal costs;
(c) London *Evening Standard* – interviews with stallholders selling under the Westway;
(d) *Best* – an interview with a woman who had an autistic son;
(e) *Time Out* – interviews with 'Guardian Angels' on the London Underground.

LEARN TO EARN

Just a word on opportunities for new journalists. The bad news for beginners is the same as for any profession; in a recession many staff journalists are being made redundant, so most staff job vacancies and freelance commissions will go to them because of their experience.

But the good news is that whatever the economic climate, EDITORS ARE ALWAYS ON THE LOOK OUT FOR RELIABLE WRITERS WITH FRESH IDEAS – those who can come up with new angles on old subjects.

The way for potential staffers to get a foot in the door is to take *any* job they can get on a newspaper/magazine, let's say as a secretary, research clerk, whatever. Once on the inside you will see opportunities to be grabbed. A reporter is suddenly off because of illness or a domestic crisis, so you offer to cover a story. If you turn in a PROFESSIONAL write-up the editor will remember you next time. Thousands of journalists started this way.

For freelances the situation is similar in that editors remember the ones with the most original ideas, and it's those people that will be contacted should the publication's regular contributor be unable to produce the goods.

And for potential freelances and staffers, THE ORIGINALITY OF THEIR WRITTEN PIECE OFTEN DEPENDS ON THEIR CREATIVITY AS AN INTERVIEWER. Interviewing is an essential element of the talent of journalism.

By the way, you don't need to be in a union to become either a staff or freelance journalist.

Aiming for a job on the staff of a magazine or newspaper is certainly worthwhile. It's staffers who get the plum jobs – because they have all the machinery and funds of their publication behind them.

Invites to interview the top celebrities are sent to newspapers and magazines – so are free tickets for top sporting events, first nights and pre-release films.

You may aspire to being in a war zone where THEY have guns in their hands and all YOU have is a pen. But you can't have this high excitement as a war correspondent as a freelance. You have to be a staffer.

As for the type of person you need to be, I rather liked a comment made by the surgeon and writer Han Suyin: 'How much sincerity, idealism and spiritual integrity belongs to those who follow the hard working, austere trade of journalism. I found them more balanced, less prima donnaish, and more tolerant of fresh ideas than people in my profession.'

One of the delights of being a journalist is that, unlike the person-in-the-street, you have access to stars of stage, screen and sports arena, plus business magnates, politicians, presidents, royalty and the aristocracy. It must be the top profession for meeting interesting people.

TYPES OF WRITE-UPS

There are two main types of write-ups you interview for – NEWS ITEMS and PROFILES. And both of these are subdivided.

NEWS ITEMS are divided by length – a short one is a News Story, a lengthier one is a News Feature. One is just a longer version of the other. (A news story would appear in the first three pages of a newspaper, while a news feature would usually be on a later page inside.)

PROFILES are divided not by length, but by format. And *nota bene* or you could be confused – the two sub-divisions of profiles are Q&A and Feature – that same word 'feature' again. But don't confuse it with the News Feature. Throughout this book, when I talk about a FEATURE I mean a News Feature, NOT the feature format of a profile. And so do editors.

The difference between these two types of profile formats – Feature and Q&A (Question and Answer), is that Q&A has no narrative, it's merely a list of questions and answers. The other is a mini-biography written as a story.

The best ones have an angle, a nucleus of news – perhaps the celebrity has just moved house or got married. Or what most celeb profiles do is focus on the author's new book or rock singer's disc, or sports star's latest race.

TYPES OF INTERVIEWEES

One of the delights of being a journalist – an intensely lonely profession – is that interviewing brings you into contact with people.

There are roughly three types of people you'll interview:

1 'Ordinary', non-famous, members of the general public. They could be a witness of an accident, the victim of a mugger, the hero of rescue attempt. Or perhaps an official of a new club or support group – or a man raising money for charity – or a woman who has had a frightening experience that you need to know about for a feature.

2 Specialists in any field about which you happen to be writing. You may need someone such as a cardiologist to give you statistics on the number of heart transplant operations carried out in Manchester in the last twelve months.

3 Celebrities These will be stars of screen, TV, concert platform, stage, or sports arena, authors of top-selling books, performers on top-selling discs. Additionally, there are royals, aristocrats, big business barons and that ilk. These are the sorts of people upon whom you do profiles. Those in categories (1) and (2) you mostly need for features.

OVERVIEW

To give you an idea of what you're in for, let's now have an overview of the various components of interviewing, plus a few of the problems:

Sell it first *The professional journalist sells the piece first. Otherwise, there's no point in doing either the interview or the written piece.* I give you tips in Chapters 3 and 21.

Angle *Before the interview you need to decide on a saleable 'angle' for your finished write-up.*
This is so you don't waste precious interview time asking random questions. Each question needs to be planned so the answer is part of the structure of the saleable piece you're writing. (Which doesn't mean you can't change the angle if a better one occurs while you're doing the interview.) Chapter 2 gives you an example of how an idea for a feature is born and followed through.

Approach *First of all, you've got to get the subject to agree to the interview.* Don't ever assume you have some sort of divine right to extract information from people.
There are all sorts of psychology involved here. You've decided on the person you NEED to interview to discover whether the serial killer had a violent childhood, or the most up-to-date statistics on the numbers of baby seals slaughtered, or why Deborah Drama took such an unusual part in her latest film. If the person who has the information says they won't grant you an hour of their time, you're in trouble.

Always be prepared for a 'No' – you can't assume they WANT to be interviewed. After all, it's an imposition on their time. YOU'RE the one who needs the info, for a feature for which YOU'LL be paid.

Your subject, if he's a novelist, for instance, will get publicity for his latest book; but unless the interviewee is promoting a book/play/film/disc he gets little apart from an ego trip. As beginners, you're not into cheque book journalism. Learn how to persuade them in Chapters 6, 7 and 8.

Preparation   *This will take far longer than the interview itself, and is just as important.*

You will see from the contents list of this book that preparation covers several chapters and you don't get down to the actual interviewing till Chapter 13. Successful interviewers complete all the preparation stages I cover. Remember, you get only one opportunity for that interview. You can't go back and do it again.

As it's a 'one-off' (much of it 'an unknown factor' because you can't know what the interviewee is going to say), the more work you do beforehand the more confident and professional you will be during the actual face-to-face meeting. This means the more able you will be to write up the finished piece – the *raison d'être* of the interview anyway.

Note-taking   *Everyone speaks faster than longhand can be written.* Unless you can write ACCURATE shorthand at 180 words per minute, you can't note down ALL the person says. The solution is a dictating machine/tape recorder. More on this in Chapter 12.

Questions   *First define exactly the information you need, then plan the questions to get that info.*

Perhaps that sounds simplistic – but too many beginner interviewers let the subject go off at a tangent and come away without the facts they need.

The minute you begin the interview you START WRITING THE STRUCTURE OF THE FEATURE OR PROFILE IN YOUR HEAD. Develop the ability to think on two levels at once –

asking questions and mentally shaping the piece as you go. NEVER LOSE SIGHT OF THE WHOLE AIM of the interview – THE PIECE YOU WRITE AFTERWARDS.

You can formulate your questions by a never-fail process of lateral thinking called C.Q.R. which I'll show you in Chapter 2, or think them up without it.

Most of them should be open-ended, i.e. can't be answered with a simple 'yes' or 'no'. You can't sell a piece consisting of a list of 'yeses' and 'noes' – especially if it's a profile – you want to bring out the subject's personality. Chapters 10 and 11 give you help on questions.

AT THE INTERVIEW

Control *You must be in charge of the interview all the way through.*

Never let your subject take over or you won't get the information you came for. Chapters 13, 14, 15 and 16 deal with this – and the next three points.

Demeanour *Your demeanour and appearance are important – they determine the way in which your interviewee reacts to you.*

What you should present to your interviewee is an amiable, knowledgeable person who's GENUINELY INTERESTED IN WHAT THEY HAVE TO SAY. Whether or not you feel it is immaterial. Your position of strength is that most people like to give their opinions.

Nerves *Never forget that subjects always feel they're in the hot seat.* You must be aware of this and put them at their ease or fear could make them clam up and you'll come away empty-handed.

You can't fully appreciate what it's like till it's happening to you. You'll conduct far more successful interviews once you've discovered what it's like to be on the receiving end. So try and find at least one other potential journalist/

interviewer and practise on each other. (See Chapter 9 for more tips on this).

Problems   *There are many, many problems when one person is trying to extract information from another.* The interviewee could be taciturn, or even violent; maybe you can't get them to talk, maybe you can't stop them; the Big Name may be a right prima donna; they may contradict themselves; you may have to interview with other people present, you may have to ask 'delicate' questions; they may ask for money; they may try to harass you sexually. I tell you how to cope in Chapters 7, 15 and 16.

Write-up   *It's quotes – comments out of their mouths – that you need for the finished write-up. And remember, you must never put into quotes anything they didn't actually say.*

Whatever form it takes, what makes your write-up extra interesting are the words actually spoken by the interviewee – and these should be in inverted commas, of course.

If you put between quote marks anything not actually said by the interviewee they can sue you for misrepresentation. It's entirely up to you to structure the questions so they come out with quotable quotes. That's another reason to make most of the questions open-ended.

The profile or feature you eventually write depends on how well you do your preparation. During the interview never lose sight of the piece you'll ultimately write.

Before the interview you'll have structured your profile or feature in outline, decided on the salient points you need to emphasise – and the only person who can supply this emphasis is your subject. If you come away without that info, then you've failed. And you won't sell your piece to an editor – WHICH IS THE WHOLE POINT OF THE EXERCISE.

Now I've given you a general overview of interviewing.

I give you a map, but YOU have to make the journey. It may all seem a bit daunting now, but don't let that throw you. I promise you, your confidence will develop by reading this book. And practising interviewing with friends will also help.

EXERCISE

Without re-reading this chapter, write down the difference between an article and a piece of journalism such as a news feature or a profile.

CHAPTER 2

Step-by-Step Process for a Profile

- Choose the person
- Ring an editor
- Contact your subject
- Preliminary research (Books)
- How to Create Questions
- Preliminary research (People)
- True story
- Markets
- Exercise.

THIS CHAPTER focuses on how to prepare an interview of someone on whom you are going to write a profile.

There are five steps you must carry out BEFORE THE INTERVIEW for every PROFILE you write:

1   Discover an interesting/famous star or specialist to profile.
2   Sell the idea of the profile to an editor, or at least get a promise from him/her that he/she will read it. (There's no point in doing all the work of researching, interviewing and writing if you're not going to be able to sell it, is there?)
3   When you've found an editor who has expressed a definite interest, contact your potential interviewee to make an appointment to interview them.
4   Research – find out as much as you can about the person you want to interview.

5   Prepare questions to ask them using the C.Q.R. method.
C.Q.R. stands for CREATING QUESTIONS FROM
RESEARCH. This system will give you a graph which plots
various trains of thought and throws up questions to ask at
the interview. Readers of my first book will already know
the basic method, but not as used to formulate questions.

The best way of covering the five steps is by using the
example which follows:

1   Choose the person

You're preparing to do a profile on Emma Talisman, a novelist
whose book was nominated for the Booker Prize, but didn't
make it.
So why bother with her?
Only your hunch. Let me give you the background.
Every year a short list of the titles of the six novels nominated
for the Booker Prize are published in the quality Press. You're
interested in books, so you noted what was said about this
year's authors. Five of them had quite interesting mini-
biographies, the sixth, that of Emma Talisman, was pretty
ordinary – nothing to tempt a journalist to interview her.
The book nominated was her novel *Culture Conflict*. It was
about an English woman married to a Chinese diplomat – 'a
deeply moving, cerebral account of East married to West', said
the review in the *Guardian*. Which didn't reveal a great deal.
So, a rather mundane biography plus a rather brief review
doesn't add up to a pulsating, saleable idea for a profile. Well
it didn't for the vast majority of journalists. Practically nothing
had been written about this woman. Why? asks your journalistic curiosity.
On impulse you ring the publisher of *Culture Conflict* and ask
for the publicist, 'What do you know about Emma Talisman?'
'Not a lot,' is the uninspiring answer. 'In fact no more than
you've seen in the press. This is her eighth novel, none of the
others were earth-shakers – steadyish sellers, but never in the
top league.'
'What about Ms Talisman herself?' you persist.

'Again, not a lot. Even as her publishers we know little about her, except that she's not very co-operative with the Press.'

Not sure whether you're annoyed or intrigued, you ask for her address.

'Oh, she won't allow us to divulge that.'

A blank wall. You say 'Thanks,' and hang up.

You see two alternatives. Either some journalist has followed up Emma Talisman and discovered she really is such a boring or insignificant person there was nothing to write about her, or all journalists came up against the same brick wall and didn't bother to try and get around it.

You sense a challenge. You get *Culture Conflict* out of the library. It is such a sensitive, compelling and incredible story you can't stop reading till you reach the end. None of the reviewers could have been awake!

Set in China in the last century, it tells of a Swiss woman who married a Chinese mandarin. The husband dies in hospital of typhoid. As widows have no status in China, the woman was expected to commit suicide. When she refused, her in-laws conducted a vendetta against her. The book ends with her jumping over a cliff.

Your hunch is that the book is so empathetically written it's possibly semi-autobiographical.

So your investigative motivation (that exists in all good journalists) takes over.

2 Ring an Editor

First, risking all, you ring the features editor of a glossy monthly women's magazine. Now profiles, like features, have to have an ANGLE. In the case of profiles the angle is usually the celebrity's forthcoming book, film, concert, whathaveyou. You don't do a profile on a celeb 'just because they're there', if you see what I mean. All pieces of journalism need an angle, a focal point, or they won't sell to a publication.

In this case you haven't got a forthcoming book to hang it on. As the Booker Prize is for published books, *Culture Conflict* was in print before it was nominated, and that's months ago now.

So you tell the features editor your hunch. (You ALWAYS ask for the features editor by NAME – very important this. You find out what her name is by looking on the masthead of the publication – or asking the switchboard operator.)

You ask: 'If I'm right and the novel *is* semi-autobiographical, would you be interested in a profile?' She says: 'Yes, but I'm only agreeing to read your profile, not publish it; and I won't even read unless your hunch is right.' Tenuous, but the good news is that she DID say she'd look at it. And you immediately confirm this arrangement to the editor in writing.

3   Contact your Subject

You then sit down and write to Emma Talisman, care of her publisher. You explain how deeply impressed you were with *Culture Conflict* and how honoured you'd be if she'd kindly talk to you about it. You truthfully explain that such-and-such quality magazine were interested in her story IF IT WAS TOLD SENSITIVELY AND NOT AS THE GUTTER PRESS WOULD HANDLE IT. You invented the bit in capitals, but you've a strong feeling she might react more favourably to this approach. You don't tell her your hunch, of course – it might frighten her.

4   Preliminary Research (Books)

You don't wait for a reply before you start the research. You now:

1   Read all the other books she's written.
2   Read everything in your Press cuttings file on her.
3   Ask in the library for her biography. (There isn't one.)
4   Look her up in *Who's Who*. (She's not mentioned.)
5   Get a presspack from her publisher (this is pages of personal details which include a biography and bibliography, a sort of CV).
6   Create a C.Q.R. graph to discover questions to ask her.

There's actually a great deal more to PREPARATION, but I'll cover that later in the book.

. And meanwhile, you've just received a letter from Emma Talisman herself saying she's agreed to meet you.

Facts you've found through research about Emma Talisman:

- Born in China of British parents;
- Leisure activity – sailing;
- Marital status – single;
- Now lives – Bourne Marsh, Hants;
- First seven books written under name of Jane Smith;
- Novels 4, 5, 6 and 7 are a series;
- Books set in China, Tibet, Bangladesh, India, Turkey;
- 8th novel *Culture Conflict*, written under name of Emma Talisman, was nominated for Booker Prize, but didn't get it.

5 How to Create Questions

You are now going to do a C.Q.R. – Create Questions from Research. Take the largest piece of blank paper you can find (A3 if possible), and write her name in the centre. Around it put points learned through the research you've just carried out, plus every other source you can think of. I could only come up with eight facts.

When you're doing C.Q.Rs. you surround the name with ALL the facts you've gleaned from ALL your research sources. With the forthcoming interview in mind, put them in a logical order. You will want to start with the easy questions, where your subject doesn't need to think too deeply and can relax, and work up to the more substantial questions later when you and she have a warm rapport going.

Circle each fact and link it separately with a line to the nucleus. Each satellite is now the start of a train of thought.

Let your stream of consciousness flow. Ask questions in your head. Note down, in as few words as possible, every query you have connected with the topic in the satellite circle. Include solutions – these will be your assumptions, of course, and will need to be checked with the interviewee.

Write them in a string, i.e. circle each point and link it with a line to its predecessor as your train of thought progresses. The linking line is to help you keep track of each 'train' because your graph will become very untidy as you keep adding points.

To discover more points, keep asking: 'What happens if
. . . ?' – good old cause and effect.

When you've exhausted every avenue, get a NEW notebook.
List (leaving space for replies), each satellite point in logical
sequence. Under each topic, list just a couple of trigger words
to remind you of the related questions.

If you'll now look at the graph you'll see I've started a series
of questions – and I continue here.

Look at No. 1.

1 Start with the sort of basic questions you'd ask anyone –
'What did your father do?' 'What did your mother do?' 'What
schools did you go to?' As at least one early school was probably in China, you could ask: 'Do you have an anecdote or
two to tell about your school days?' 'What were your best
subjects?' 'What college did you attend?' 'Did you go to university?' 'Did you take a degree?' What else could you ask?

....

2 You want to know: 'Where did you learn to sail?' 'Were
you in your college team?' 'Did you ever think of making a
career out of it?' Milk each point dry before going on to the
next. What else would you ask?

....

3 'Have you ever been married?' Plan alternatives – if she
says 'No', you could follow with: 'Did you decide you preferred
a career to marriage?' If she says she's a divorcee or a widow,
you can ask about her ex-husband and does she have any children? What else could you ask?

....

4 'I looked up Bourne Marsh and discovered it's one of the
smallest and remotest villages in England. Is that the reason
you came here?' 'It must be ideal for being able to concentrate
on writing – is it?' 'Don't you feel cut off from the commercial
world of publishing?' What else could you ask?

....

About now she will be really warming up, so get on to the
main angle of the profile you will write, her writing career.

C.Q.R. FOR A PROFILE

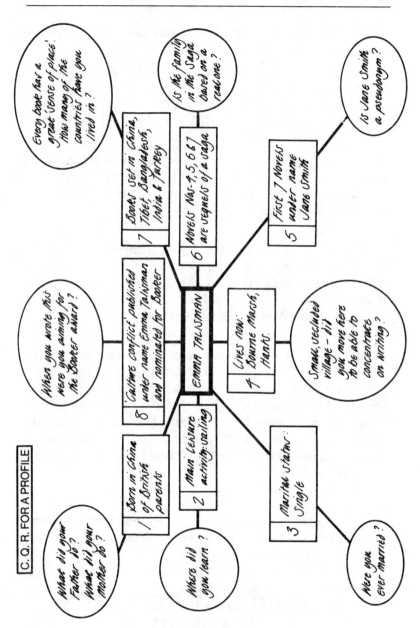

Central: EMMA TALISMAN

1 Born in China of British parents
— What did your father do? What did your mother do?

2 Main leisure activity: writing
— Where did you learn?

3 Marital status: Single
— Were you ever married?

4 Lives now: Bourne Magna, Hants.
— Small, secluded village – did you move here to be able to concentrate on writing?

5 First 7 novels under name Jane Smith
— Is Jane Smith a pseudonym?

6 Novels Nos. 4, 5, 6 & 7 are sequels of a saga
— Is the family in the saga based on a real one?

7 Books set in China, Tibet, Bangladesh, India & Turkey
— Every book has a great 'sense of place'. How many of the countries have you lived in?

8 'Culture conflict' published under name Emma Talisman and nominated for Booker
— When you wrote this were you aiming for the Booker award?

Don't jump straight into asking about the Booker, make it easier for her by starting at the beginning:

5 'Is Jane Smith a pseudonym?' 'Why change it after seven books?' 'Is Emma Talisman your real name?' 'What motivated you to start writing in the first place?' 'What are your biggest problems when planning plots?' What else could you ask?

....

6 'Is the family in the saga based on a real one?' 'You will have regular readers of the sagas. How did they react when you wrote *Culture Conflict*, which was a radical departure in style?' What else could you ask?

....

7 'Every one of your books has a tremendous "sense of place". How many of the countries you depict have you lived in?' If she says 'None', then ask her how she does her research. If she says: 'All' or 'Some of them', ask if she also worked in those countries. What else could you ask?

....

8 Here comes the high point of the interview. By now you will have a really productive rapport going with her: 'When you wrote *Culture Conflict*, were you aiming for the Booker Prize?' 'How much credence do you put on literary prizes?' 'Did being nominated for the Booker boost sales?' Then the Big One – 'The story is so vivid and vivific it comes over as autobiographical. Is it?' 'What motivated you to write it?' What else could you ask?

....

Now you see how plotting a C.Q.R. generates questions. It's a 'stream of consciousness' exercise. You note down every question that comes into your head.

PRELIMINARY RESEARCH (PEOPLE)

Street Level Research will help you here. One morning I was outside the Royal Opera House queuing for rehearsal tickets.

I asked other people near me in the queue: 'What would you ask Emma Talisman?' I got a useful list: 'Who or what inspired the books?', 'What sort of childhood did she have?', 'What does she do when she isn't writing?', 'How much of her own experiences are there in her books?', 'What's her general philosophy on life?' (much more on Street Level Research in Chapter 3).

TRUE STORY

The example I give you for the profile C.Q.R. is a genuine one (but I've changed the names, locality and some of the circumstances as she is still too frightened to be identified). It is a graph I dug from my oldest files. I want to show beginner interviewers that if they keep their antennae switched on, there are many instances where they have equal opportunities with established professionals.

By leaving the really 'heavy' questions till well on into the interview with 'Emma Talisman', I first built up a trust between us as we talked. It was then I discovered my hunch was right – that *Culture Conflict* was autobiographical.

She had married a Chinese diplomat in China. After three years of marriage he was killed in a car crash coming home from his office.

Widows officially 'do not exist' in some remote parts of China even today. As a wife belongs to her husband, on his death she has no purpose and becomes a non-person. Her very traditionally-minded in-laws expected her to 'do the right thing' and commit suicide. When she refused they started a vendetta against her.

Even as the mother of a son she had no value because there were plenty of relatives in the extended family who could look after him.

The situation became unbearable when she was kept prisoner in her own house and was terrified to eat because the food sent in was poisoned. Even though she wasn't allowed to see her son, she was torn between him and self-preservation.

Eventually, weak through lack of food, she climbed through a window and ran down to the nearby docks, stole a sailing boat and sailed to a large port. There she bought a ticket on the first ship that left. It was going to India.

Penniless in India she hitch-hiked her way north to Kashmir and into Tibet; not because she wanted to go there but because that's where her lifts took her. She spent over a year trekking and working her way overland via Bangladesh, Turkey, and Greece, to France where she crossed the English Channel in a fishing boat.

Once in England she put herself at the mercy of the Red Cross who fed her till she got a live-in job. She became a nurse to an elderly man who lived in Bourne Marsh, Hants.

Here her luck turned. Her patient had no relatives and when he died, a year later, he left her his house and a little money. His generosity allowed her to turn to full-time writing.

She had lived there ever since under an assumed name, terrified her in-laws might catch up with her. To try to exorcise her traumatic experience her creative spirit compelled her to write a fictionalised account of it. *Culture Conflict* took six years to write.

So this was a case where fact was indeed stranger than fiction.

MARKETS

No successful journalist starts interviewing without a market in mind. Until you've decided on the readership you're aiming at, how can you know what to ask your interviewee apart from generalities that apply to all publications? The type of publication you select dictates many of the types of questions you ask.

Another good reason for studying the publications you choose to offer your work to – it always triggers pertinent questions because you see the way features and profiles have been handled by other journalists they have published.

If you're writing for a glossy monthly woman's magazine you'll ask different questions from those you'd ask for a men's glossy or a weekly newsmagazine.

Good Housekeeping and *Woman's Journal* are two publications that would be interested in a profile on an intelligent, not too young, woman novelist with such a traumatic experience.

You could also interest *Writers News* or *Writers' Monthly* in a feature on how Emma Talisman used her own experiences in her book.

And another market – the *Independent* or *Guardian* are just two newspapers that like emotive pieces on women achievers.

So that's three potential sales from one interview.

EXERCISE

1 Choose a subject.
2 Write it in the centre of a large piece of blank paper.
3 Do a C.Q.R. graph.
4 Put it away in a drawer for a week.
5 Take it out and see how many other questions you can devise.
6 List the questions as trigger words.

CHAPTER 3

Step-by-Step Process for a Feature

- Idea
- Preliminary research (Books)
- Market
- Angle
- Listing interviewees
- Questions to ask
- Preliminary research (People)
- Street level research, how you start
- Examples
- Approaching the editor
- Example of an Outline Letter
- Exercise.

HERE'S THE WHOLE PROCESS of how a professional journalist can develop a FEATURE. I say '*can* develop' because, of course, each feature is unique – but the step-by-step procedure of producing them all is similar – and they're not all that different from the five steps for a profile (see start of Chapter 2). This is one I had accepted by a monthly women's magazine. But if you already have a topic for a feature don't skip this chapter, as it tells you how to develop YOUR idea.

1   Idea   One way to get an idea for a feature is to contact all the magazines you'd like to write for. Ask them for their Features List. This outlines, edition by edition, the major subjects to be written about for the current year.

The list is produced for the advertisers so they know when an edition has editorial relevant to the products they want to sell. Any of the subjects listed could trigger a feature in your mind.

What follows is how I got one particular idea – without the aid of a Features List.

Sitting on a bus behind a man and woman, I couldn't help but hear snatches of their conversation. 'I just couldn't cope with marriage – the wedding and everything – I just couldn't cope,' said the woman. He put his arm around her, I could only hear his odd word, '. . . love you . . . together . . . cohabitation . . . contract . . .' She didn't reply immediately. Then, as she began: 'Well, I don't know . . .' I had to get off.

That's all there was. But it set me thinking. As all professional journalists do, I keep an eye on what is published in magazines and newspapers, and I'd seen hardly anything written about cohabitation contracts.

It was a subject that affected both women and men, and was indeed a national issue. So plus point No. 1 was that the subject would have a wide reader appeal. And plus point No. 2 was that it could certainly be emotive if it included lots of quotes from people who'd had relevant problems. Emotion has a big reader attraction.

What did I know about cohabitation contracts? Not a lot. All I was certain of was that they were a list of commitments to each other which can be drawn up and signed by couples who live together but aren't married.

2 Preliminary Research (Books) I went to my Public Reference Library. I asked at the counter: 'I want to find out something about cohabitation contracts, please.'

The librarian was very helpful. 'Well, you can look in the Humanities Index, *The Times* Index, and I think I read something about it in the *Guardian* a month or so back, so try their Index too. They're upstairs, when you get to the top they're just to the right of you.'

She came round from behind the counter. 'And over there are a couple of books on living together, there's also a Living

Together Information Pack, would you like that?' Librarians are marvellous at pointing you in the right direction.

I sat down in the library with this lot for a couple of hours noting down anything interesting. Whilst I was doing this the librarian brought me a five-month-old copy of *The Times* that carried a feature on cohabitation contracts.

After reading everything, I noted down titles and the whereabouts of all the books, papers and indexes so I could refer to them later if I needed to. (More on book research in Chapter 5.)

At home I dug through my Press cuttings files for anything relevant. All professional journalists build up Press cuttings files by clipping news items, news features and profiles on subjects that can be of use in the future.

3 Market Something else I learned from references to back copies of newspapers – the topic hadn't been over-exposed. I could find only one feature about cohabitation contracts in the last year. And there certainly hadn't been one on the *Guardian* Woman's Page (an ideal subject for them). Right, there was one market. If the feature wasn't going to be too long, I'd approach them. However, if I eventually accumulate a lot of material for the feature, then one of the up-market women's magazines would be a better bet as they'll take longer, in-depth pieces.

And listening to the news on the radio, I hear a report on new proposals for adoption laws in the light of the growing number of couples who want to adopt children but aren't married. Apparently, more than a third of couples who live together aren't wed. I'm not interested in the subject of adoption, but the information about unmarried couples is relevant. To me it means there's a lot of people who, being cohabitees, will identify with my topic and could be affected by the existence or not of a cohabitation contract. I scribble this in my notebook.

Later I CHECK it. I consult my card index of information sources and telephone the Office of Population, Censuses and Surveys (071 242 0262). They tell me that in Britain, 1.2 million couples cohabit without being married. Do you see the relevance? 2.4 million people could be directly concerned, so a feature would certainly appeal to them – a goodly number, and this doesn't include a few million more people who aren't cohabitees, but would still be interested. I make another note to include this statistic in my outline letter to the editor when I'm trying to sell the piece. (More on Marketing in Chapter 21).

4 Angle As the subject is rarely written about, its sheer NOVELTY is its strength from an editorial viewpoint. But that doesn't mean it can do without an angle. I decide to focus on the question, 'Should cohabitation contracts be a short-term prelude to marriage? – Or a long-term alternative?' I could well change this as I research further; I might discover a better angle.

5 Listing Interviewees No piece of journalism 'lives' until it has quotes from people involved with whatever subject is chosen. Yes, I could just write about the legalities of cohabitation contracts. But that would better be written by a lawyer – SO IT WOULDN'T BE JOURNALISM.

No, what I was planning was to interview as many people as possible and get their viewpoints. I'm going to write a 'human interest' piece. (For a profile, too, you will be able to write a far more interesting/saleable piece if you interview people connected with your celeb than if you spoke only to the Big Name.)

- **Specialists:** for starters, the obvious ones I need to talk to are a counsellor at Relate (formerly the Marriage Guidance Council) and a solicitor.

    Perhaps a psychologist would also be useful, but I know many of them dislike journalists, and anyway their ethics (like those of Relate counsellors) forbid them to reveal names of couples who have cohabitation contract problems, or any of their clients for that matter.

    So I decide to rely on a psychotherapist friend. I know she won't give me any names either, but if she has a client or two with a problem in this area, she'll tell me the gist of them and I can invent the names. At least it'll be authentic.

I can get quotes from other specialists from books they've written. I make a note to research books by doctors and counsellors.

● **Non-specialists:** all my other interviewees will be couples, or halves of couples (i.e. people who've experienced what I'm writing about or who have suffered or benefitted from its effects).

6 Questions to Ask   I sit down with a large piece of paper and do a C.Q.R. graph (Create Questions from Research, see page 27).

7 Preliminary Research (People)   When doing features you'll need to do **Street Level Research** – that's questioning members of the public. I advise this for two reasons:

a   to sound out the topic I've chosen to write on. To see what reactions I get. If enough people look bored when I mention Cohabitation Contracts (or whatever topic) then I'd have to drop it and go on to something else. You can't expect to bring to fruition EVERY idea you think up.

b   to start getting quotes for the feature. With some people I'll contact them later for a longer discussion. Street Level Research is a series of mini-interviews.

(For profiles, Street Level Research can throw up additional questions to ask.)

How you start   Street Level Research can be literally in the street. I memorise most of the questions thrown up by the C.Q.R., and start at street level. A journalist's job is to track down people who have one or more of the experiences you're writing about, plus people who know people who do, plus people who at least have something pertinent and interesting to say even though they're not either living with someone or married.

Being beginners, and perhaps reticent, you will start with people you know – friends and relatives. That's OK. You'll then add friends of friends and work colleagues. And that's OK, too. But when you get to writing at the rate of a new profile or feature every week, those people will get pretty fed up with you if you always seem to be quizzing them. Anyway you need fresh ideas, not predictable ones.

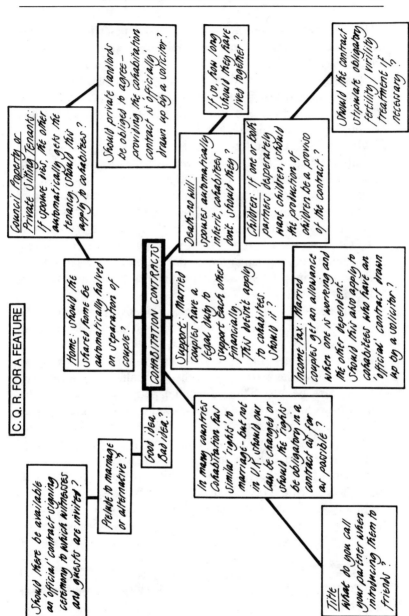

C.Q.R. FOR A FEATURE

COHABITATION CONTRACTS

Council Property or Private Sitting Tenants: If spouse dies, the other automatically gets the tenancy. Would this apply to cohabitees?

Should private landlords be obliged to agree – providing the cohabitation contract is officially drawn up by a solicitor?

If so, how long should they have lived together?

Should the contract stipulate obligatory fertility/virility treatment if necessary?

Death-no will: spouses automatically inherit, cohabitees don't. Should they?

Children: If one or both partners desperately want children, should the production of children be a proviso of the contract?

Home: Should the shared home be automatically halved on separation of couple?

Support: Married couples have a legal duty to support each other financially. This doesn't apply to cohabitees. Should it?

Income Tax: Married couples get an allowance when one is working and the other dependent. Should this also apply to cohabitees who have an 'official' contract drawn up by a solicitor?

Good idea. Bad idea?

In many countries cohabitation has similar 'rights' to marriage – but not in U.K. Should our law be changed or should the 'rights' be obligatory in a contract as far as possible?

Prelude to marriage or alternative?

Should there be available an 'official' contract-signing ceremony to which witnesses and guests are invited?

Title: What do you call your partner when introducing them to friends?

So you chat to people at bus stops, in doctors' waiting-rooms, supermarket check-out queues, hairdressers, the badminton changing-room – anywhere you've a captive audience for a few minutes. Understand, these really are chats, they're not full-scale interviews. Those come later when you've enough pointers to indicate that the feature is definitely worthwhile writing and potentially saleable.

Of course you don't do all this on one day. Or even one month, perhaps. It's an ongoing process along with chatting about other features you have in the pipeline.

Notice, you haven't started writing anything yet apart from notes. Neither have you contacted an editor. The professional journalist SELDOM WRITES ON SPEC, BUT SELLS THE PIECE BEFORE IT'S WRITTEN. All you've done so far is planning and preliminary investigation to see whether or not you can find enough interesting material by research and interviewing to tempt an editor.

Your method is the same as that of a private detective. He UNOBTRUSIVELY chats to hundreds of people. Journalists do the same. BUT YOU CERTAINLY DON'T LET ON THAT YOU'RE A JOURNALIST AT THIS STAGE, or say you want to INTERVIEW them. It's the words 'journalist' and 'interview' which scare people. That can make people clam up, as the gutter press have given journalists a bad name. People will also ask embarrassing questions about where your write-up's going to be printed – and you don't know yet.

If you talk to enough men and women, you're bound to discover a few with views on cohabitation contracts that will make a worthwhile contribution to your write-up.

Before I say any more, a SERIOUS WORD OF WARNING. Sad to say, in this day and age, it is always best to approach strangers carefully – ESPECIALLY IF YOU ARE A WOMAN.

Whenever I speak to someone who has an interesting point to make I note their name in my notebook (and phone number if possible), plus the place and date I spoke to them. I will contact them later for an interview.

In the following examples I tell you what I did. This, of course, is to show you what YOU could do.

Example 1

A typical approach would be something along the following lines. You might be at the hairdressers or at the gym where you work out. I'm in the changing-room of my local swimming pool where I go every other morning. A woman, a stranger, is near me – we're both drying off.

ME (lying! this is merely an opening gambit): Did you hear that thing on the radio last night about cohabitation contracts – very interesting?

SHE: No, but I was out, so I wouldn't have. Pity – I'd like to have heard it. What did it say?

ME: Just went on about the advantages and disadvantages – didn't say they were good or bad. (I don't want to colour her opinion beforehand, so I make it non-committal.)

SHE: Personally I'm dead against them, unless there's children involved. I mean, the whole point of living together is that it's free of commitment – built on love and trust. If they want something in writing they may as well get married.

ME: Right. (To encourage her and show I agree.)

SHE: I've lived with someone for nine years and we seem to manage OK. But I've got this friend who's desperate for somewhere to live now her other half's just died – all this on top of her grief. They lived in a nice little flat, which he owned and was in his name, of course. Now he's dead she doesn't have any claim on the place because they're not married.

It went to his son who's in Tasmania and he hasn't seen for 15 years – didn't even come back for his father's funeral. The son doesn't want the flat so has told an agent to sell it as quickly as possible and send him the money. My friend's got to leave by the end of next week, she hasn't a hope of finding enough to buy it. I think it's inhuman of the son – but there it is.

ME: Yes. If there'd been a cohabitation contract which stated the flat went to her on his death, she would have been protected.

SHE: Yes, it would have been a good idea there. The same thing happened to a gay friend of mine too. Couples should look at all the OTHER contracts, then they wouldn't need a cohabitation one.

ME: What other contracts? (NB: even if you know the answer, you still ask questions as though you didn't, because people may add one or two facts you hadn't thought of.)

SHE: Well a will mostly, that'd take care of the other person when one dies. But also the house purchase contract, the mortgage – whose name it's in, and the joint bank account, that sort of thing.

ME: And tenancies for rented homes can be in both names.

SHE: Yes, that too. These contracts should all be looked at thoroughly.

And there I have some good quotes for my feature. I nip into the loo with my notebook and rapidly scribble down what she said before I forget her exact words. But before I do that, if I think she's more to say of any relevance, I say: 'Look I'm in a bit of a hurry now, and I'm sure you are too, but could we talk some more about this because it might help a friend of mine who's in a bit of a fix. May I have your phone number?'

Her comment on her gay friend also gave me an idea for an additional feature. There'll probably be a gay publication that would buy a piece on cohabitation contracts from the homosexual viewpoint. You never sell a good idea only once. Always be on the lookout for other markets.

Example 2

On another occasion, a writer colleague, Alan, rang me to ask the name of my agent. After I'd told him I asked him: 'What are your views on cohabitation contracts?'

ALAN: Tricky area. On a practical level I think they're a very good idea, but on a personal level I'd be too embarrassed. I mean you can't go up to a woman with a ring in one hand and a fifty-page contract in the other, can you? It's almost as if you're courting disaster, pardon the pun.

ME: So you've never had one?

ALAN: No. I've lived with, ahem . . . quite a few women, but never made it that official. Are you writing something on this then?

ME: Probably – depends on how many decent quotes I can get.

ALAN: Why don't you ask cohabitees who already live together how they'd feel if their partner suddenly suggested a contract? I can give you a couple of names. Society's set up by men – on their terms – a contract might be the only security the woman's got. I mean, she can't rely on him to be faithful. If he walks off because she's getting a bit long in the tooth, she's left with absolutely nothing to show for a fifteen-year relationship.

ME: Yes, thanks, that's a good idea.

ALAN: And how about couples that've broken up? You could ask them if the existence of a contract might have held them together.

ME: Right. Thanks – I'll do that.

That's another example of Street Level Research. Can draw blanks, but equally, can be very fruitful. It's very much 'testing the water' to see if there's enough indignation, passion, grief, caring among people on this particular subject. Because it's emotive comments that 'make' a feature.

And all this is meeting people – one aspect that makes journalism such a fun thing to do.

8 Approaching the Editor The idea's now been sloshing around in my head for a few weeks. I've got names of about nine people whose varied viewpoints will collectively make a saleable piece. Apart from one, they know nothing about the feature or that I'm a journalist, of course. And nothing is yet written. There's no point in doing the next stages; all the hard work of interviewing people and writing it up, if I'm not going to be able to sell it, is there?

Looking at all the material I've collected, mentally adding yet-to-be-gathered comments from the psychotherapist and other specialists, I decide there'll be enough for a 1,500 word feature. So this tells me my market shouldn't be a newspaper but a monthly women's magazine. I'm an experienced journalist so I have a couple of editors I can approach whom I know might be interested. But let's say I'm a beginner.

I go to the largest newsagents I can find and skim through the women's magazines to discover first which editors will currently even consider unsolicited contributions (work they haven't commissioned, i.e. asked the journalist to write). Analysing all the up-market women's monthlies it seems nearly all might be interested in cohabitation contracts, as long as the piece is written up in their house style, of course. I make a note of all the possibles – title, editor's name, address, phone number.

I choose one and write the editor an OUTLINE letter. As by now I've a pretty clear idea of the structure of the entire feature, I can describe it so she can see it on the page. I'm enthusiastic – it's a novel subject.

In a week or two the editor rings me and says: 'Yes, this sounds OK – I could be interested – let me see it.' Notice, she's made no commitment. But great! at least she's promised to read it. Now we're getting somewhere.

For a profile the approach to the editor is the same, only different (how's that for clear communication!). As with my guidelines on features, I tell you what to actually SAY to the editor on the phone in a later chapter.

OUTLINE LETTER

Ms Judy Writewell,
Features Editor,
'New Woman',
24 Bloggs Street,
London W17 1DE.

Dear Ms Writewell,

MUMS' ARMY

Would you be interested in 750 words on seven women who served in London's HOME GUARD during World War II? Their own experiences include at least two that were 'beyond the call of duty' and were awarded medals for bravery. All seven have hair-raising anecdotes of real incidents during the Battle of Britain and other periods of the war. These include taking part in the capture of a German pilot whose plane was shot down; of manning(womaning?) an Ack-Ack gun when the gunner was wounded by shrapnel; and of one licence-less ARP woman driving a truck loaded with sandbags to save a blazing building next door to a petrol station.

I will interview each woman, also their superior officers where possible. In addition, I will get quotes from retired Fire Brigade and Police officers who were with them during the Battle of Britain.

Included in the piece will be statistics showing the number of women who served in the early 1940s, plus a brief spotlight on the role of women in today's Civil Defence organisation.

Both my grandparents were in the Home Guard during the war, together with several of their brothers and sisters, so I have many sources of personal reference.

The Battle of Britain started in August 1940, and this is an anniversary piece for your August edition. As this is only four months away, may I look forward to an early reply, please. I enclose a stamped addressed envelope.

Yours faithfully,

Paragraph 1 – Who, What, How, Why, When, Where.
Paragraph 2 – What quotes will be included.
Paragraph 3 – Relevant background information.
Paragraph 4 – Writer's relevant experience.

EXERCISE

Street Level Research is something you'll need to do a lot of. And again – remember to have all your wits about you BEFORE approaching a stranger. Psychopaths do not have a card around their necks saying BEWARE!

1 Choose a topic (not an embarrassing one) – make it something in the headlines that everyone is talking about like a current disaster or royal event. You're not going to write it up, this is merely an exercise in approaching strangers.

2 Go somewhere where you are among strangers – not a party or similar social occasion because people expect to talk to others. Go and stand in a bus queue, on a station platform, in a supermarket checkout queue or sit in the waiting room of a vet, doctor or dentist. You could try the changing-room at a sports centre – and there are other places, of course.

3 Strike up a conversation with someone the same sex as you on the subject you've chosen. Pretend to not know much about it – the more questions you ask (count them) the more points you score. By the way, you're cheating yourself if you speak to someone you know because you won't be learning how to cope with strangers.

4 Do the exercise several times to see how high you can score. Each time you do so it'll be a little easier.

CHAPTER 4

More on Research

- Interview stoppers
- Quotes are the icing
- The star
- Family and friends
- Taboo list
- The specialist
- Know the answers
- Exercise.

NOT ENOUGH CAN BE SAID about research – it's as essential to the interview and the final write-up as paper is to the writer.

Creative journalism is the basic Who, What, Where, When, Why, How (discovered by research), made vivific by quotes (obtained at interviews). A person who writes a piece derived merely from their own experiences and book research is an article writer or essayist. A journalist is a FEATURES writer and uses these as background only. Additionally, he goes out and interviews people to get their opinions and anecdotes.

I find the research as fascinating as the writing, and am sometimes so carried away by accumulating more and yet more facts, I'm in danger of gathering enough material for a book rather than a feature or profile!

INTERVIEW STOPPERS

Interviewees have been been known to terminate a meeting in the first couple of minutes if they discover that the interviewer has made little or no effort at research beforehand.

Let's list a few examples:

- 'Good afternoon, Paddy Ashdown. What party do you represent?'

- 'Good afternoon, Steven Spielberg. What films have you directed?'
- 'Good afternoon, Princess Diana. What countries have you toured in the last year?'
- 'Good afternoon, Jeffrey Archer. What's the title of your latest book?'
- 'Good afternoon, Rupert Murdoch. How many newspapers do you own?'
- 'Good afternoon, Nigel Mansell. What make of car do you drive?'
- 'Good afternoon, Madonna. How many times have you been in the Top Twenty?'

Don't giggle. Some of these are true!

Of course you can't answer all of them off the top of your head – but you CAN look them up. Any information that is look-upable is never asked by professional journalists. You find out as much about your interviewee as you can BEFORE you interview them.

And you can bring tears of fury to the eyes of politicians and other public figures by asking them a question they've just answered in the House, on TV or in the Press. It's insulting to them and merely proves you are inept and not worthy of an interview. Time is always precious for public figures.

QUOTES ARE THE 'ICING'

You don't interview Big Names for 'ground-level' information but for the 'icing on the cake'. Let's take that analogy. You make a good, solid fruitcake from basic ingredients such as butter, flour, eggs and dried fruit. This equates with your good, solid profile fashioned from basic information you've got from research – where they were born, their nationality, where they were educated, how many times they've been married, how many kids they have. Now for the icing – the 'extra' that turns the pretty ordinary cake/profile into an exciting, intriguing, SALEABLE final product. The icing equates with previously unknown details from the mouth of the Big Name.

An exception to this rule is when you're testing a point of accuracy. You ask politicians a crucial question when you KNOW the answer they gave last time, in an effort to see if they contradict themselves.

THE STAR

For a profile on an actor, say, you need to have seen a number of his films or plays. You also need to read the reviews and perhaps books about the actor and be *au fait* with his current personal circumstances plus details of his recent movements. Otherwise, you won't be able to say: 'I was interested in the comment you made on Radio 4 last week. You said you had many scripts sent to you – could you expand on that?' or, 'Because of the success of your current play, do you fear you'll always be offered the villain's part in the future?'

I promise you, if you interview an established actor and say: 'I confess I've never seen you in any plays or films . . .', you will only antagonise your subject and you could even be shown the door.

Journalist Jean Rook was a master at this. She said: 'I do nine-tenths of the work before the interview. I never ask anyone "Is this your third marriage?" – I find out before I go.'

I was speaking recently to Clarissa, a leading drama teacher who's had many of the top stars through her hands. She'd just had lunch with a Big Name who had been nominated for an Oscar in his latest film. Clarissa told me: 'He's so modest about the nomination – genuinely didn't expect it, and is convinced he doesn't deserve it. What he's most proud of is how his wife and mother feel – and what he most dreads is being interviewed by the Press.

'He said he's trapped by a clause in his contract obliging him to be co-operative with the Press to get publicity for his films. But he'd give ANYTHING to refuse all interviews. He's been "done" by many of the leading newspapers and magazines and he's so sick of the same old questions *ad nauseam*. He said: "If I'm asked once more did Olivier influence your work? I'll go through the roof."

'He wants to know what happened to creative journalists. He said: "If I played Iago the same way other actors did I'd soon be out of a job. How is it that journalists can serve up the same old stuff that's been written before, and get away with it?" '

FAMILY AND FRIENDS

For a really in-depth profile with pithy anecdotes you don't stop at interviewing the Big Name. You seek out her/his family, friends, neighbours, hairdresser, ex-schoolmistress, tennis coach and work colleagues *et al.*

How do you find these people? You research your subject's autobiography/biography if they have one, plus features/ profiles about them already published in magazines and news-papers. You chat to people who work/worked with your sub-ject. You discover the school/college they attended, go there and talk to teachers who might also give you addresses of your subject's parents and classmates. Use your ingenuity for more sources.

Courtesy   On the whole, if you're courteous, considerate and quietly enthusiastic about the person you're profiling, then people who know him will be willing to chat about him for a few minutes. And that's all you need. Some are quite flattered that you seek them out.

OK, some will tell you to get lost. But you must be prepared for this – you can't win them all.

You'll very often get: 'Oh I don't know much about him/any more about him, you should speak to so-and-so, they were at drama school together/in the same Scout troop/lived in the same street/married his sister.' And there you have a lead. Most people are genuinely happy to help you with research.

It's diplomatic to ask the Big Name's permission to speak to his wife/uncle/best friend. Play it by ear.

It's useful to build up your picture of the star BEFORE you ever come face-to-face with him. You've seen plays he's been in, read other people's profiles on him, looked him up in the

Spotlight Casting Directory (see Chapter 6) and spoken to his agent, interviewed people who know/knew him. Research is sometimes exciting, sometimes tedious, but always intriguing as you piece together the vast jigsaw puzzle of this person's life. Then, when you meet him you'll come over as well informed.

He will either take it that you've paid him a compliment by doing your homework or that you've maliciously meddled in his private life! You won't know till you meet him. One of the risks journalists take daily.

Openers 'Hello, Mrs Smith. Forgive my intrusion, but I understand you're the mother of actor X. I'm writing a piece about your son and would be grateful if you could spare me a few minutes, please. I'd merely like a couple of anecdotes about his childhood, schooldays, first job, anything at all really. Can you remember his telling you when he got his first part in a school play? What was it? . . .'

'Excuse me, sir, am I right in assuming you style/used to style the hair of X? Good for your reputation, eh? Can you recall any amusing incidents about him, for instance his views on men dying their hair? . . .'

'How do you do Mr Callboy. Can you remember X playing at your theatre? What was he like – punctual or invariably dashing in at the last moment? . . .'

TABOO LIST

Journalists are sometimes restricted in what they're allowed to ask. When the Big Name is available for interview, all the writers who are going to meet him/her could be given a list of 'taboo' subjects by the publicist. These are topics that the star won't talk about. These could be the death of their child, for instance, or their six months in a clinic for alcoholics, or how much they received for the film.

Also on that list will be 'safe' subjects that CAN be talked about. So those are the parameters. Although ALL the interviewers have to work within these bounds, it shouldn't follow that all the profiles read as though they came from the same pen.

INTERVIEWING IS AN INTENSELY CREATIVE PROCESS. Editors are looking for profiles that are ORIGINAL.

And an interviewee whose eyes will glaze over when presented with yet another banal question, will usually respond enthusiastically to something they've not been asked before.

When you're given that 'Taboo and Safe' list, take it to your library and dig deep. Remember that research on a superficial level will have been done by the other journalists with the same list.

You look up references to the 'safe' topics – could be holidays, say. You know from the Presspack information that your Big Name usually takes his family to Provence. Nothing terribly original in that. But familiarise yourself with what's been written about Provence for tourists – winkle out some of the less known interesting facts about the area. Then include questions about those when you sit down and do a C.Q.R.

THE SPECIALIST

Much of what I said about research for celebrity profiles in Chapter 4 also applies to features about topics (for example photography or arthritis).

Specialists are similar to celebs in that you don't waste their time with unnecessary questions. And although you'd interview the Big Name for a profile and the specialist for a feature, the process is the same. Get the basic facts from book research and the topical, profound details from the interview.

The specialist in particular often welcomes an unpublished writer's request for an interview like the bubonic plague. Usually scholarly, s/he cannot face the anticipated battery of inane questions. So refuses to meet them.

The answer is to talk intelligently on their discipline when you ring for the appointment (see Chapter 8). Then their reaction to you will be entirely different. People don't despise the neophyte for their ignorance – it's UNNECESSARY ignorance they abhor.

You can't ask intelligent questions unless you UNDERSTAND the job they do. Do you know the difference between a mammogram and a mammograph? – or *sub judice* and *in camera*? – or a film director and a film producer?

KNOW THE ANSWERS!

A colleague of mine had a golden rule: 'Never cross the interviewee's threshold without knowing at least 50 per cent of the answers.'

So why interview, you ask? Well, if the questions are not banal ('Are you married?'), but controversial ('So how many people are going to be made redundant?'), to get the answers in THEIR words. Their 'voice' is what gives the piece its individuality and authenticity. It's something that can seldom be invented effectively.

Another benefit of knowing some of the answers beforehand: it gives you a more positive concept of the piece you will write afterwards. Therefore you're better able to control the interview and steer it in the direction you want it to go. With some of the answers already noted down, you will be better able to focus your mind on additional questions that will get you quotable anecdotes.

And another reason to research thoroughly – don't think your subject will meet you cold. They will probably have done their homework and be well clued up.

Before you're very far into the interview an interviewee realises from your questions whether or not you've adequately researched, in other words how weak and vulnerable you are. If you appear shaky then they could think: 'Great, I can lie low, I needn't reveal X.' Whereas, if faced with an obviously genned-up interviewer their thought is more likely to be: 'Well I'd better come clean about X because s/he probably knows about it anyway.'

EXERCISE

Without re-reading this chapter, list five points you should know about a celebrity *before* you meet them for the interview.

CHAPTER 5

Sources of Information

- Public reference libraries
- Encyclopaedias
- Humanities Index
- Law about photocopying
- Newspapers
- Information Bureau

- National Newspaper Library
- Definitive book
- Acknowledgement
- Exercise.

TAKE THIS ON BOARD: a journalist doesn't need to know anything about anything; s/he merely needs to know WHERE TO FIND OUT. Being an investigator is a paramount journalistic skill.

The adage stressed on Creative Writing courses 'Write about what you know', is a restraint journalists do not recognise. Journalists can write 1,000 words on ANY subject. They aren't restricted to their own experiences. Research and interviewing specialists make journalists instant experts on ANY subject.

I spent many years in the trade and industrial Press. I built up a general knowledge of stationery and office equipment, aluminium and pharmaceuticals. Those were my subjects – so I was thrown when I was asked by an editor in the farming trade Press to write a feature on future trends in combine harvesters. The chap who was supposed to write it was in hospital on a life support machine, and the editor needed it in three days.

Knowing nothing about the subject, I got a couple of recently published books out of the library and got the rest of the information from people at the three factories that made combines. In two days I became an expert on modern combine harvesters. Any other journalist could have done the same.

PUBLIC REFERENCE LIBRARIES

There is no subject that hasn't been written about. Public reference libraries contain books, articles, maps, periodicals, information packs, pamphlets, leaflets, microfilm, microfiche and many other pieces of data. They are available to everyone – and should be a journalist's second home. As a taxpayer, the libraries service is something you've already invested in.

If we all used the libraries more, perhaps the local councils wouldn't keep reducing the hours. There's a whole weekday when my nearest library doesn't open at all.

If you're not already a regular visitor to your Public Library, don't be intimidated. Just go to the desk and say: 'I'm looking for some books on iridology.'

The librarian won't laugh or fall over in a faint. She'll look up iridology on a computer screen, give you titles of all the books they have, with their reference numbers, and point you in the direction of the right shelf.

ENCYCLOPAEDIAS

And don't forget the *Encyclopaedia Britannica* – one of the journalist's best friends. So are the other encyclopaedias in the library – *Everyman's* (which I asked my parents for as a 21st birthday present), *Macmillan's Family* and *Chambers* among them. Plenty of subjects have their own encyclopaedias, for instance: psychology, religion, biography, science fiction, criminology, medicine, world history and superstitions.

And these are supplemented by hundreds of dictionaries, yearbooks, annuals, gazetteers, directories, guides, handbooks and manuals on specific subjects.

HUMANITIES INDEX

Once you've investigated the Humanities Index you'll wonder how you ever managed to function without it. I use it a great deal. It's a vast collection of published features and articles on topics as diverse as abortion and zoogeography.

The Doomsday Computer (every fact on mankind) is another useful source, and so are all the *Who's Who* series which includes *Who Was Who*.

LAW ABOUT PHOTOCOPYING

Most libraries have a machine, so you can copy the occasional page to take home.

NB: copying more than three per cent of a modern book is illegal as it contravenes the Copyright, Designs and Patents Act 1988. When I say 'modern' I mean one that is in copyright. Generally speaking, an author's copyright lasts for his lifetime plus 70 years after death and a publisher's copyright 25 years from publication.

This is fair. Unrestricted copying from books, journals and periodicals would deter authors and publishers from producing the material in the first place.

NEWSPAPERS

Your Public Reference Library should also have *The Times* Index. It lists features printed in the newspaper under subject. Started in 1790, it is published monthly and has yearly summaries. The *Guardian* also started one in 1986.

Also in the library will be a collection of editions of your local newspaper. Additionally, you can see copies at the newspaper's office, and they should have specific cuttings, listed under subject, that they'll let you look at.

INFORMATION BUREAU

In days of yore every journalist's first call was the *Daily Telegraph*. For 40 years they would answer ANY question you put to them, and the information was free. I've done many stories with their help. But in 1989 they withdrew their Research Service because they were losing money.

An independent company took over the service. They're called appropriately The Information Bureau – 071 924 4414. They charge you £5 plus the time it takes them to look up the information you want. They will find out anything for you from the date of the very first World Cup or the Spanish Inquisition, to full-scale biographical details of personalities in sport, politics, business, TV and film. Plus a great deal more.

NATIONAL NEWSPAPER LIBRARY

If the Public Reference Library is the journalist's second home, then the National Newspaper Library is the third.

It's at Colindale, North London – Tel: 071 323 7353 – and the service is free.

This invaluable organisation keeps copies of every British newspaper published from when it was first launched. They're magnificent for people wanting back-numbers when writing a follow-up to more or less any national event – also for anniversary pieces.

They also have weekly periodicals (British and Commonwealth) – PLUS comics. A great information source. All you need do is just turn up with some form of identification (passport, for instance). Their hours are 10AM to 4.45PM every day except Sundays. They can even have the newspapers you want to read ready for you when you arrive if you give them 24 hours' notice. By the way, you can't take them away, this is purely a reference library. But they do have photocopying machines.

DEFINITIVE BOOK

To help you I can't recommend too highly the definitive book on this subject *Research for Writers* by Ann Hoffmann (paperback, A. & C. Black). It's as valuable to a journalist as his dictionary and *Roget's Thesaurus*.

ACKNOWLEDGEMENT

When you use the information you seek in your write-up, please acknowledge your source.

- It's a courtesy – after all they have done the work of collecting those facts in the first place.
- It gives credence to the piece you're writing.
- It's an example to young journalists coming after you. You will appreciate acknowledgements by future writers for work you've originated.

It's not difficult. All you need write is something along the lines of: 'As Prof. L. Bunsen-Burner said in his book *Trial and Error*, "The heart rate is accelerated by a factor of eight during an attack" ', or ' "No government will ever be brave enough to make nicotine illegal," said Max Blather MP, speaking on *Panorama* on 24 June 1994.'

EXERCISE

Select a subject that intrigues you – you could try female circumcision or mercenaries.

Go to the Public Reference Library and check to see if there's a piece on it in the Humanities Index.

Also check *The Times* and the *Guardian* indexes.

Then discover how many books the library has on the subject.

CHAPTER 6

How to Contact Them

- Stars of Stage, Screen, Sport
- Authors
- Royalty
- Specialists
- Councillors
- Politicians
- Embassies
- Exercise.

So, IN THE FIRST PLACE, how do you discover how to make contact with the person you wish to interview?

STARS

Most stars of stage, screen and radio are 'unavailable' most of the time. A variety of human buffers are paid to keep away the general public and journalists so the Big Name can get some privacy. But the famous surface when they want to promote a book, play, film or disc. Then the interviews are up for grabs.

For appointments with and information on actors of stage, screen, TV, and radio you contact their agent. This also applies to production people such as directors, choreographers and stage managers.

How do you discover who their agent is? You ring Spotlight: 071 437 7631. They have two huge volumes – the Casting Directory and the Production Directory, both updated annually. The first one contains the names and photos of several thousand actors and actresses including children, drama school leavers, stunt men/women, and registered disabled performers. The second lists production personnel.

Spotlight staff will look up the agent's phone number for you free of charge.

Should you want to contact the agent of a comedian/enne or variety performer, you phone *The Stage* weekly newspaper: 071 403 1818.

Alternatively there's the directory *Artistes & Agents* (updated annually), which lists agents and personal managers, promoters, Press and publicity agents among many other contacts, along with the names of over 10,000 artistes. It's published by Richmond House at around £16.

Sports Stars For a start, phone a magazine that specialises in the specific sport.

AUTHORS

To contact authors: send to their publisher a letter addressed to the author in a sealed envelope. On it you put a postage stamp and the author's name. The publisher will add the address and forward it. Of course, you'd enclose a polite covering letter asking the publisher if they'd mind doing this. The same goes for journalists you want to contact, except that you send the envelope to the editor of the publication their piece was printed in.

ROYALTY

One of my students came into class in a fury: 'I missed the chance of a lifetime. I went to the theatre last night and what do you think? Only two boxes away was Princess Diana. I could kick myself. I was so spaced out staring at her – she really is lovely – it didn't occur to me to interview her. I didn't think of it till I got home.'

Now she was being unrealistic. There's no way she could have interviewed Princess Diana even if she had thought about it at the time.

All royalty have bodyguards (armed!) who wouldn't let anyone get within speaking distance.

And even if it was possible to speak to her it would be extremely bad manners. Princess Diana wasn't doing a public duty. She was there on her night off. The same applies to a celeb you meet in the supermarket or at a party. They are entitled to time off the same as every one else.

If you need to speak to any member of the royal family go through the official channels. You ring the royal Press Office: 071 930 4832.

SPECIALISTS

Perhaps you need a historian or a horticulturist. Hopefully they've written a paper on the subject you're interested in, so you write to them care of the editor of the publication in which it appeared.

Suppose you need a medical expert such as a radiographer or cardiologist. Merely ring your local hospital and ask the switchboard for the name of their Consultant Radiographer/ Cardiologist (get the spelling and pronunciation of their name right). Then ask to be put through to his/her secretary.

If you need a specialist but don't have a name, then contact the appropriate professional society or trade association; for example, the British Medical Association would help with doctors. If you don't know the name of the professional body then ring the trade or specialist magazine, e.g. *Architectural Review*, *Shooting Times*, *Computing*.

NB: Professions are a virtual maze of titles. Be sure you get right the one that precedes the name of YOUR interviewee. Check it with their secretary before you speak to them: she's as anxious as you are that it's correct.

This is vital when you're acknowledging a quote in print. It's also important to the person concerned. Additionally, if you get it wrong you'll lose credibility with your editor.

By the way, when at the actual interview you can always ask experts for names of their colleagues whom you can interview. That way you'll get a good variety of quotes on your topic.

COUNCILLORS

If you're writing up a local or national political issue, you could have difficulty in getting to speak to an official of any seniority. Since a number of 'public embarrassments', in 1989 a law was passed that prohibits anyone working for a local council, and earning over £10,000, from speaking to the Press regarding politics. This can be a real brick wall. They are protected by law from being interviewed and are quite twitchy about it.

But all is not lost. Most local councils do have PR departments which WILL speak to you. Their staff have been carefully briefed as to what they can and cannot say to the Press. So, you might not get Alderman Blather or a council official, but you will get quotes, and you attribute them to 'a spokesperson': 'An official Westminster Council spokesperson confirmed that . . .' You don't write 'Westminster Council PR dept confirmed that . . .' as this is much weaker. Unless, of course, you're shooting them down in flames: then you can say 'Alderman Blather was not available for interview, but the PR department said . . .' That's very crushing!

The PR departments of most councils are pretty good, and usually helpful. They're mostly staffed by bona fide journalists – though you will come across the occasional council who will put you on to 'good old Walter', as long as he's not busy making the tea.

POLITICIANS

To contact an MP you ring the House of Commons on 071 219 3000 and ask for his or her office.

EMBASSIES

They're all in the telephone directory.

For instance I rang the Press Office of the American Embassy in London (071 408 8074). They have a very helpful PR department.

The ex-Commonwealth countries do too. So you should be able to get some decent quotes if you're on the track of, say, two Brits who met with fatal accidents in New Zealand, or a tug-of-love story where the English mother's taken the child to her parents who emigrated to Canada.

Every working journalist has a card index of useful addresses and phone numbers of reference libraries, picture libraries, the PR depts of trade associations, royalty, film companies, church organisations – you name it. And the Public Reference Library has the *Directory of Associations* – an invaluable tome.

EXERCISE

1 Look in today's newspaper.
2 Discover someone famous whom you consider interesting.
3 Go to the Public Reference Library and look them up in *Who's Who*. (They won't necessarily be in there.)
4 Work out how you would contact them should you need to.

CHAPTER 7

Setting up the Interview – Pre-planning

- Plan feature/profile first
- Be professional
- Suppose they refuse?
- Nervous neophyte celebs
- Should they see write-up?
- Blackmail
- Is it convenient?

- Preliminary facts
- Duration of interview
- Venue
- Sexual harassment
- To write or phone?
- Rivals
- Exercise.

BEGINNERS are never prepared for the problems of getting an appointment for an interview.

Too many student journalists get great ideas for a feature/profile and diligently do the research. Then, when they're ready to do the interview, they ruin the entire project because they can't get the person/people to agree to see them.

If my intended interviewee refuses to meet me then I won't get the quotes I need to make the write-up saleable.

It's important HOW I handle the initial approach. I must immediately come over to them as an amiable person they are happy to talk to; AND I HAVE ONLY THE ONE PHONE CALL TO MAKE THIS IMPRESSION.

I NEED to interview them. I must remember that they don't need to be interviewed. All the benefits are for me, I'm the one who will be paid for the feature/profile, not them. So I have a big persuasion job each time I approach anyone for an appointment. I mustn't be belligerent or superior – I have no divine right to extract information from anyone.

Just put yourself in their shoes for a moment. How would you feel if a total stranger said he wanted to question you – especially if he said he was a journalist? Personally, my first reaction would be to erect the barricades!

PLAN IT

Before I pick up the phone to arrange an interview for a profile/feature I need to be completely prepared. I don't want to dither and sound like a twit. So I work out three things:

1   APPOINTMENT STRATEGY,
2   SKELETON OF WRITE-UP,
3   LIST OF QUESTIONS.

1 Appointment Strategy   This is to organise you, to ensure you have all the basic information. You won't get far applying 'scatterlogic'. Write down the journalist's old friends, Who, What, Why, Where, When and How in a single column. Then fill in the answers:

WHO   (name of person you want to interview);
WHAT   (you are going to write – news story, feature or profile);
WHY   (to publicise their film, help further their cause, give you info on a project they're working on, be one of a few people from whom you're getting opinions on X, etc);
WHERE   (suggested venue for interview, their place or yours?);
WHEN   (time and date you'd like to do the interview);
HOW   (method of getting hold of them? [Get number from phone directory, ring their agent, manager, secretary, publisher, theatre, House of Commons, etc.])

Don't go ahead till you've sorted out that lot.

2 Skeleton of Write-up   It helps enormously if you can see the shape of the feature/profile BEFORE you ring them. This saves you being vague on the phone, which irritates people.

You know your subject and your angle. On a single page sketch out most of what you're going to write (gathered from the mass of research you've done), and the order in which it will be written.

Now you can see the gaps in your information. THIS is what you are going to get from your interviewee. It is vital that you KNOW what you want to know from them. Only rank amateurs mumble and splutter over the phone when they ring to make an appointment (or at any time), because they haven't thought out beforehand what they want to ask.

3 List of Questions   Still preparing to make the appointment for the interview, I take a large piece of paper and list down the left-hand side the main questions I want to ask. Just jot down a few trigger words for each, leaving space on the right-hand side for their answers.

But shouldn't you ask the questions at the interview? Yes, but it could be that they're leaving to emigrate to Canada in the next hour – so I need to be prepared to interview them there and then on the phone.

A face-to-face interview is by far the best method – it lasts longer (so I've time to explore my topic in more depth); I can study their body language (which helps me control the interview better); and they can take time to think about their answers. But a phone interview is better than nothing – be prepared to compromise. From their viewpoint at least, they'd probably be more relaxed because they're not eyeball-to-eyeball with the questioner.

You're now nearly ready to make that crucial first phone call. But don't do it yet.

To help allay your natural nervousness just THINK THROUGH what you're about to do. Don't blindly rush in relying on hope to conquer panic. If you merely play through the sequence in your mind there'll be less surprises, so you'll be better prepared. Remember, this applies to EVERY phone request for an interview.

Let's say you're ringing an agent. So you're sitting by the phone with your 'Appointment Strategy', 'Skeleton Structure' and 'List of Questions' ready, plus your diary. You psych yourself up by taking a deep breath and telling yourself you're going to:

(a) pick up phone;
(b) key number of TV company that screened *London's Burning*;
(c) ask for Publicity Department;
(d) say: 'Hello, please may I have the name and number of the agent who handles James Hazeldine who plays Mike Wilson?'
(e) They will ask: 'Are you a journalist?'
(f) I reply: 'Yes.'
(g) Then they'll happily tell me what I want to know.

It's as simple as that. It's what publicists do all day and every day. (Refer back to Chapter 6 for how to find an agent.)

BE PROFESSIONAL

Be organised, disciplined, precise, polite – IN OTHER WORDS, PROFESSIONAL when making your request for an appointment: 'If it's convenient, I'd like to talk to you on the 15th or 16th of next month.' Be positive – 'I think you'll find our discussion interesting – the piece is for *Best* which has a million readers.' Then follow with: 'It'll be publicity for your play', or 'will further your cause'. Point out the benefits to THEM.

Ask for a time convenient to them – also duration (perhaps an hour) – it's up to you to leave them with the impression that you're a professional, a nice guy, and the interview will be an enjoyable experience.

SUPPOSE THEY REFUSE?

Suppose your proposed interviewee refuses?
After all it's an imposition on their time. Your subject, if

he's a novelist for instance, will get publicity for his book; but other interviewees will get nothing but an ego trip (and that's only if they enjoy the interview). You're not into cheque-book journalism.

Generally, if your tone of voice is quiet, confident and courteous people will feel they can trust you and will comply. But you can't always rely on this. So you need a contingency plan should they refuse to give you an appointment. In other words you need to be prepared for a 'No', and be ready to try and persuade them.

Why might they refuse?

For starters there's the usual problems of life – an illness, a bereavement, a marriage break-up. Then again they may just be going away on a business trip, to a conference, on holiday. Or, probably the most usual reason, they're just too busy. So be prepared to offer to see them in two or three weeks' time. Have your diary at your elbow.

Or it may be fear. And this could be the reason be they a celebrity, specialist or 'ordinary' non-famous person. Daily the gutter press verbally slaughter somebody or other. These are the spectaculars that catch the eye and are remembered.

Because of this odious treatment, a phone call requesting an interview could terrify the ordinary man/woman-in-the-street. The thoughts of their comments, and worse, their NAME appearing in a newspaper puts some people into shock. And they're scared you'll take their skeletons out of their cupboards, dress them in naughty underwear and parade them on the front page (even if you only want to talk to them about their dog winning a prize at the county show or how they raised £100 for the Neighbourhood Watch street party).

NERVOUS NEOPHYTE CELEBS

Then there are the people who react to: 'May I interview you?' very similarly to being asked: 'May I paint your portrait?' They're overcome by equal feelings of flattery and fear. Quite often they're in show business, on the second rung of their career and have been interviewed before.

Most of us like to have people paying us attention, listening to our opinions and to us talking about ourselves. They feel that's the good news. Their bad news is knowing it's going into print and they have no control over what's written.

So they say they'll let you interview them if you'll let them see what you write before you send it to the publication. In other words – if they can vet it.

SHOULD THEY SEE IT FIRST?

Celebs and 'ordinary' people   If you agree you're in for big trouble. They will always change it, invariably taking out the most lively bits because they think it shows a lack of dignity or something.

They will also mull over it for so long that you won't get it back in time to meet your deadline. And another hazard – it's not unknown for an interviewee to send a professionally-written piece to an editor under their own name and get the fee for themselves.

So don't ever let them see it. What you say is: 'It's against editorial policy to let you see it. It's just never done. Please believe you can rely on my professional integrity not to libel you or make you look ridiculous.'

Specialists   It's a *very good idea to let a specialist see your finished write up – or at least let you read the technical bits to them over the phone.* You will get added Brownie points from your editor because you can say it's been verified.

By the way, experts such as scientists, historians, horticulturists *et al.* need chasing. Many boffin types work in an environment where time doesn't exist. You send them your write-up and they could put it aside to be attended to 'later'. Then other papers get put on top of it and your piece sinks without trace.

Tell the specialist, courteously, in your covering letter, that the editor has asked to have it by Friday. You have another copy, so if they could kindly read it by the day after tomorrow, you will ring then and they can read you any necessary alterations.

BLACKMAIL

Some Big Names – and small names – refuse to give you an interview unless you can guarantee that the write-up will be on sale in the newsagents in a quality publication.

Unless you have a commission, you can't do this. But if you've got an editor to agree to at least read your piece, then you can truthfully say to your potential interviewee: 'There are no guarantees in publishing, but I CAN tell you that an editor has said he's definitely interested.'

Never tell them the title of the publication. Say 'a glossy monthly', or 'one of the quality nationals', or 'a leading specialist magazine'. If you mention a title your subject might ring the editor to discover when the piece will be published.

IS IT CONVENIENT?

When you ring always ask if it's a convenient time for them to talk. They could be rushing to catch a train, watching their favourite TV programme, just about to make love. If your call interrupts them they'll be annoyed, and that's not the frame of mind in which you want them. If they say it's not convenient, you follow with: 'No problem, I'll call again. Would four o'clock be OK?'

PRELIMINARY FACTS

In that initial phone call, find out as much as you can about your potential interviewee.

- It leaves less to ask during valuable interview time so you can use that hour more fully.

- These discoveries suggest questions to ask you hadn't previously thought of. See how long you can get them to chat.
- You have prior warning of their temperament, accent and mode of speech. Even from one phone call you can often tell if they're arrogant or shy, taciturn or a jaw-me-dead.

DURATION

Unless they state they can give you only half an hour, whatever, it's up to you to decide for how long the meeting will last.

Interviews can be any length. But those you'll be tackling as a beginner will probably be between 20 minutes and a couple of hours.

Psychologically, 'about an hour' is the best length to ask for if you're doing a profile. It's long enough to make them feel important and not as scary as 'How on earth can I keep talking for two hours?'

When you make the appointment, it's best to be a trifle vague: 'Oh, I reckon something like an hour should cover it.'

Compile as many questions as you need. If you want more time, after an hour together you should have him chatting and revealing away so profoundly that he won't notice the clock.

This doesn't work for show biz people whose agents monitor the time, or for business executives who have frantic work schedules. But even they can forget the clock. It's up to you to develop that valuable rapport where s/he won't want to stop talking to you.

VENUE

It's better to visit your interviewee at their home rather than they come to you:

- They're on their own ground so will feel more relaxed.
- You can observe their domestic environment, which is very useful for a profile (traditional or quirky furnishings/decor,

affluence, they are/are not gardeners/cooks/hobbyists/animal lovers).
- They'll travel first class if they come to you – and *you* pay the fare.

Ensure during this first phone call that you get their FULL address. And don't be afraid to ask how to get there: it's unprofessional to arrive late.

Of course, if they live at the other end of the country from you, ask if they're ever likely to be in your neck of the woods – or perhaps in a large town midway. Journalists living in London are on to a good thing – many authors and show biz stars have to visit the capital to see publishers or producers.

In Public   You could meet in a pub – but this can be noisy (tapes pick up and often increase extraneous noises), and you can get off-putting curious looks from other drinkers.

Best place I've found is the lobby of a biggish hotel like the Ritz in Piccadilly. It's quiet, undisturbed, and you can order drinks, (which impresses the interviewee). BUT – important this – GO AND LOOK AT THE HOTEL'S FOYER BEFOREHAND.

It's no good if it has a group playing music, caged song birds, or loud taped music as it'll drown the voice on your tape. So will other noises if it's a particularly busy lobby. And check there's a couple of secluded seats – it will be less nervous-making for both of you.

If you're seeing a celebrity it could be that you're told the venue. This could well be the foyer of a big hotel, or the agent's office. Be prepared though, you could be only one of a crowd of journalists all there for the same reason.

SEXUAL HARASSMENT

A woman (or man) alone with a man (or woman) they are interviewing is seldom at risk – but do be aware of the possibility.

As in any one-to-one situation with a person you've never met before, don't wear provocative clothes or make provocative remarks. Be polite, but at all times maintain a professional distance, similar to a doctor/patient meeting.

The situation can be a trifle hairy if a woman goes to a man's home and he starts to get fresh. I've been in this position a couple of times.

It could be that he doesn't even fancy you, but his male ego urges him on merely because you're female and he's male.

In most instances your intuition should set off warning bells before he comes on strong.

I discovered a good ploy. And do this at the beginning, don't leave it till you're dodging round the sofa. Say your husband drove you here and is waiting in the car just around the corner.

It could be, when you speak to him to make the appointment, you suspect he may make a pass when you meet. And remember there ARE psychopaths about:

(a) don't agree to the venue being at his place;
(b) don't agree to your place either (even though you could have your Black Belt boyfriend in the next room), as when he knows where you live he can always return another day;
(c) do insist the venue be his publicist's office; or
(d) the public foyer of a large hotel.

WRITE OR PHONE?

A letter to your intended interviewee takes longer than a phone call, but you do have a record of your request for your files (useful if you're working on two or three profiles/features at once). And if it isn't answered you still have the option of phoning to ask if they received it.

A letter gives your subject time to psych themselves up to agreeing to an interview.

Many older people appreciate the graciousness and complaisance of a written request as opposed to a bald phone call. And, of course, you'd be particular about your writing paper. Cheap stationery reflects the mean-mindedness of the sender. A letter is your ambassador, the recipient's first impression of you, so let it be a good one.

But speed might be vital because you fear another journalist might get to an editor before you. Right, still sketch out a letter, but use it as the script when you telephone your potential interviewee.

Example 1

Dear Mrs Smith,

I was fascinated to read in yesterday's *Chronicle* that while the new London Zoo is being constructed, the poisonous snakes will be temporarily housed in a centrally heated warehouse. The Zoo told me you will be responsible for various aspects of the reptiles' welfare, such as ordering their special food and monitoring the heat of their quarters.

The editor of XXX magazine has said he would be interested in a feature on this project, with pictures.

Although I know your time is very precious, as a freelance journalist I'd be grateful if you could please spare me an hour to talk about this.

May I look forward to an early reply as the edition the feature will appear in is not too far away. I enclose a stamped addressed envelope, and my telephone number is as above. Hoping we can meet in the near future.

Yours truly.

NB: you don't use the word 'interview' as this can be a little anxious-making to people unaccustomed to the Press. (See PRIVATE EYE in Chapter 5.)

Example 2

Dear Mr Novelist,

I have read all your novels with extreme pleasure. I am keenly interested in your themes, i.e. the salvation or improvement of one or more of the environments, such as rain forests, puffin breeding grounds.

I was interested to read a brief news item in last week's *Sunday Times* about your scheme to send cooking pots made of recycled drink cans to the flood victims in China.

As a freelance journalist I am convinced readers would like to know more about the man behind the pen. I have contacted the editor of XXX magazine, who says she would be interested in a profile on you.

Although I know your time is very precious, I'd be grateful if you could spare me an hour or two for an interview.

The time and venue will be at your convenience. I would prefer to visit you, but perhaps you may prefer to meet in a hotel in town or at my flat.

To meet the deadline I need to do the interview within the next four weeks. I enclose a stamped addressed envelope and look forward to your reply.

Yours truly.

Example 3

Dear Mr Specialist,

I was intrigued to read in the current edition of *The Lancet* that you head a team of scientists who have discovered an absolute cure for most types of insomnia without the use of drugs.

The many thousands of readers of women's and men's magazines I write for would certainly be interested in reading about this in lay terms. And more than one editor has asked me to send them a short news feature on this subject.

Although I know your time is very precious, I'd be grateful for half an hour to discuss this, please. I could be with you any day next week at a time convenient to you. I will be ringing you in a couple of days to ask if you will be kind enough to grant me an interview.

Yours truly.

RIVALS

Of course, you can't always have it your own way – you can't rely on arranging the interview in a place where you want it. Sometimes you have to go to the mountain.

A student told me he heard that MP X was going to open this new Sports Centre. 'I had a few good questions to ask him – like where the money had come from for one thing.

'When I arrived there were stacks of reporters around him and they had microphones. They were all shouting questions and I just didn't get a look in. I wanted to see him on my own, but he did his speech and left straight afterwards. What should I have done?'

I'm afraid this is the cut and thrust of reporting. This is journalism in the real world. You have to be prepared to be in there with them, shoulder to shoulder. You can use your tape recorder – hold it as close to the subject as possible.

You'll sometimes meet this situation when a famous author does a signing or an actress arrives at a first night.

I was on a BBC Radio chat programme with *Daily Mirror* reporter Geof Lakeman. I remember him saying:

'To be a journalist you have first to be a very particular type of person. Not everyone can do it, just because they were good at English at school. You have to be tough. Journalism is savagely competitive.'

EXERCISE

1   Without re-reading this chapter, think of three venues that you would use to meet your interviewee that are quiet and undisturbed – and state why.

2   Without re-reading this chapter, list five persuasive arguments you could use if they refuse to give you an appointment to interview them.

CHAPTER 8

Getting the Appointment

- Smile down the phone at the Celebrity, the Specialist, Mr and Mrs Ordinary, the Street Level Contact
- Refusal
- Tell them the advantages
- Difficult names
- Brick wall
- Confirm it
- Exercise.

SMILE DOWN THE PHONE

HALLELUJAH, we're nearly ready to pick up the receiver to ask for the appointment! But just before you dial the number, always PAUSE. With your hand ready to take up the instrument, hype yourself into the right frame of mind first. Be ready to smile down the phone.

OK, so they can't see you. But a smile does two things.

- It mentally puts YOU into 'friendly, happy mode' which helps allay your nerves.
- It affects the sound of your voice so the recipient gets all the right vibrations and isn't met with a tone that's curt, demanding or belligerent. All salesmen are taught this technique.

Keith Hall, Chief Executive of the National Council for the Training of Journalists told me he puts 'phone manner during the initial call' at the top of his list for success. 'The person at the other end can be irritated if the journalist doesn't present a sympathetic manner. Then he won't get his information. This also applies to the face-to-face interview later, of course.'

Keith Hall also stressed that being well briefed before the interview was as important. 'If you don't know what you're talking about you might well put your foot in it with your very first question.'

Are you ready? Within easy reach you have:

- appointment strategy;
- list of questions;
- diary;
- notebook;
- ballpoint.

Dial the number. Remind yourself to be friendly and confidently courteous – and smile. This is how you start:

(a) For a Celebrity

'Hello, my name's Joan Clayton, I understand you're Gloria Glamour's agent, is that right?'

'Yes.'

'I'm a journalist and I'd like to do a profile on Ms Glamour focusing on the part she's playing in *Impossible Dream*.'

That's how you start it. No waffle, straight to the point in the minimum number of words. Agents are busy people.

If they agree, they will give you a time, date and place for the interview.

(b) For a Specialist

'Hello, may I speak to Dr Brown?'

'Dr Brown's secretary speaking.'

'My name's Joan Clayton and I'm a journalist. I'm doing a piece on Obsessive-Compulsive Disorders. I understand Dr Brown is doing a survey on OCDs at the Institute of Psychiatry and I wondered if he'd be kind enough to answer a few questions, please?'

'I'd have to ask him about this. Which publication are you on?'

'I'm a freelance. I've had a word with the editor of *She* magazine, who says she'd be interested.'

'So it's to appear in *She*?'

'I can't guarantee that. But when we discussed it the editor certainly sounded enthusiastic. She asked me to write it up and send it to her.'

'What exactly do you want to know about OCD?'

'Specifically I want to focus on what causes OCD, if that's possible. From research I know there's roughly as many men with OCD as there are women, but in the case of females the obsession is usually to do with some sort of cleaning – either themselves, their children or their home.

'I understand that in some cases a prior stress such as over-work, pregnancy, childbirth, relationship problems or death of someone close is reported by patients. But underlying that is guilt of some description. That's what I'd particularly like to discuss with Dr Brown. I want to write a piece in layman's terms which could help *She* readers who identify with OCD.'

'OK, I'll ask Dr Brown if he'll see you.'

'Please tell him I'll take only about twenty minutes of his time and it can be any day next week. What days is he at the Institute?'

'Tuesdays and Fridays. I know he's full up next Tuesday, I'll ask him about Friday. What's your phone number?'

Now you can see why thorough research beforehand is vital. When asking for an appointment you've got to know what you're talking about and be able to be specific on the exact points you need clarified. Otherwise the secretary won't take you seriously. You can't waffle along saying: 'I want to know something about OCD.' You will be expected to know the basics already.

(c) For Mr or Ms Ordinary

'Hello. My name's Joan Clayton. I hope it's not an inconvenient moment to call?'

'No. What do you want?'

'I heard on our local radio this morning that you bought a valuable painting for £2 in a car boot sale. Is that right?'

'Yes – it's worth £6,000.'

'That's marvellous, isn't it? Look, I'm writing a feature on valuable discoveries in car boot sales and yours is one of the best stories of the lot. Would you mind if I came and talked to you about it, please?'

'Will you put my name in the papers?'

'Yes, but this is a nice story, isn't it? It's not as though you've done anything wrong.'

'OK then. Are you going to pay me?'

'Afraid not. Journalists don't pay for information.'

'Miss Whiplash got paid by that Sunday paper.'

'Well that's a bit different. That's one of those sensational stories. Of course, you don't HAVE to speak to me, I wouldn't want you to think that. I merely thought it would be nice to include your clever discovery along with a few others I know about. There's one chap who bought a filthy old jar covered in grime because it'd been used as a flowerpot holder. He took it home, cleaned it up and found it was a lovely old porcelain vase. He took it to Christie's who valued it at about the same as your painting. Marvellous what discerning people find in these boot sales.'

'All right then – if it's only for a few minutes.'

'How about next week – Monday perhaps?'

'Monday I go to a class – I might do it Tuesday . . .'

'Lovely, Tuesday it is. What time would you like me to come?'

'After lunch.'

And there you have it. A bit of sympathy, a bit of flattery and friendly chat, and they will usually co-operate.

Don't suggest the following day for the talk. It's too soon and will often fluster them. Give them time to gather themselves together.

And perhaps for a different story they'd need time to look up old letters or photographs – or phone a friend or two to verify dates.

(d) For a Street-Level Contact

For another type of approach let's return briefly to the Cohabitation Contracts project.

I have been compiling a list of names (with phone numbers) of people who have pertinent, and hopefully emotive, things to say.

You will remember I have already spoken to them in a casual encounter. But this doesn't constitute an interview. Now comes the crunch point – I need to interview them properly.

So I dial their number. I remind myself to be friendly, courteous and to tell them WHY I want to talk to them. As they're not a Big Name who is used to being questioned by the Press, I won't use the word 'interview' because it might make them anxious. Neither will I use the word 'angle' because they might put the wrong interpretation on it and think it's something suspicious. Keep journalistic jargon out of it.

ME: Hello, do you remember me? We were talking about cohabitation contracts at Marcia's party last month. You kindly gave me your number.

THEM: Oh – yes – hello.

ME: I did ask you at the time if you'd give me more of your views on the subject later, and you agreed.

THEM: Did I? Well, yes – how can I help you? I'm a bit pushed at the moment, I'm in the middle of getting dinner (cleaning the car, doing my kid's homework, watching 'London's Burning', getting ready to go out, etc).

ME: 'No problem – I wasn't thinking of right now. Could we make a date to meet? May I come round and see you for just a little while? You see I'm writing a feature on cohabitation contracts for XX magazine and what you said was extremely interesting. I'd like to hear more. I want to write about the advantages and disadvantages of cohabitation contracts – and of different people's viewpoints and experiences.'

THEM: 'Oh really – you're a journalist? Well yes – how about next Tuesday? Make it about 2 o'clock which'll give us a little while before the kids come home from school.'

ME: 'That suits me – what's your address?'

I repeat this strategy with all the others on my list.

I make sure I ask them where they live. It's important to come over as a professional; it helps put me automatically into the role of controller of the situation. If I had to ring back with an apology because I'd forgotten to ask for their full address, it slightly erodes my credibility.

If anyone objects or I get a straight 'No', I have to use my common sense. If they're a bit on the hostile side I say: 'OK, sorry to have bothered you,' and quietly hang up.

But if they're merely suspicious: 'I'm not sure. Why should I talk to you anyway?' I'd appeal to their integrity and altruism, and perhaps flatter them slightly:

'Well, I'm writing a feature on cohabitation contracts for XX magazine and feel the views you made were particularly valuable. The editor thought that a feature might help their several thousands of readers who are cohabiting and are having problems. What you said on couples who have children in private schools would be tremendously helpful. All I want is about twenty minutes with you – at any time that suits you.'

If they still won't give me an appointment then I'd make do with the comments they gave me on the first occasion we spoke and not use their name, but invent one.

REFUSAL

You must always be prepared for a refusal. If they object, politely ask: 'Why don't you want to talk to me? I know you have plenty of interesting things to say', or play on their ego: 'I'm interviewing several people, but you're the person who has the most important information I need.' Don't bludgeon them, it's up to you to convince them of your integrity.

Remember: THE PEN IS MIGHTIER THAN THE SWORD – AND ETHICAL JOURNALISTS DON'T USE WEAPONS ON UNARMED PEOPLE.

So if your potential interviewee demurs, concentrate on reassuring them. Let's look at a few examples:

Example 1

'I'd rather not.'
    You follow with: 'Why?'

'I know what you journalists are like. You'll distort what I say and make me look small.'

Don't jump in with: 'Oh no we don't.' You agree: 'Yes, some journalists do do this – gutter press reporters give us all a bad name. But because their features are so sensational, THOSE are the ones you remember. But I give you my word of honour, my integrity as a journalist wouldn't let me put into print anything you didn't actually say, nor would I quote you out of context. Believe me, most journalists are scrupulously careful about this, and we're just as embarrassed by those invidious practices as you are.'

Example 2

'I'm too busy.'

'I appreciate that very much. It's because you're so committed you've achieved X (whatever it is you want to interview them about). I promise not to take up too much of your time. You tell me how long you can spare, and that's how long it will be. You won't have to waste time travelling – I'll come to your office or home, whichever suits you best. And we'll do it at whatever time and on whatever day is convenient to you.'

Example 3

'I'm going to Calcutta this afternoon.'

'No problem. Could you give me just a few minutes on the phone now?'

Example 4

'I can't. I've never done this sort of thing before.'

'Do you mean you feel shy?'

'Well – yes.'

'I bet you're not as shy as I am. Just between ourselves, whenever I have to meet a stranger I get a sleepless night. But for my job I have to put on a brave face. If I don't do this feature I don't get paid, and neither will the rent. As we're both shy I'm sure we'll get on fine together. I won't be with you for very long.'

Example 5

'I'm not a very interesting person – I've nothing to say.'

'If I didn't think you were interesting, would I be ringing you? In fact, I'm speaking to a number of people, and you're the person who has the most important information I need. And I want only a few words – just an explanation of how you thought up such a clever idea to raise money for charity (or whatever). Don't you worry about what I'm going to write, that's my job.'

Example 6

'No thank you. I've been interviewed before. It was one of the worst experiences of my life.'

'But that's terrible. What happened?'

And as soon as you know exactly what bad treatment they got you can assure them that you never do this: 'I'm an experienced journalist and all my interviews have ended with a smile from the person I'm talking to. Perhaps the person you saw was inexperienced/ill/drunk. On behalf of my own profession, I can't apologise enough.' Yes, that's laying it on a bit thick – it depends on how badly you need the interview.

Example 7

'I'm still not sure. This might be a hoax.'

'Would you feel better if I gave you the phone number of the editor so you can confirm it with him?'

TELL THEM THE ADVANTAGES

In all cases describe the positive results that will be achieved by your write-up – the benefits for THEM. For instance: the publicity will further your fund-raising cause, give hope to others in a similar position to yourself, help sell your book, emphasise the credibility of your company.

One of the best ways to reassure people who're not used to talking to the Press is to explain the rules:

- I'm not going to interrogate you, just have a friendly chat.
- I'm not going to pry into your private life.
- If you inadvertently tell me something you don't want printed, you have only to say so. I'll then treat it like all the other 'off the record' comments I'm given – forget it.

BRICK WALL

Sometimes you come up against the brick wall of a straight 'No'. This is OK if seeing them isn't vital. Everyone has the right to refuse.

But suppose you need to interview Mrs Jones who lives in the flat below a man who murdered his wife. On the day the woman died, Mrs Jones heard the couple rowing. (NB: this is after the case has been heard, of course. Before that, anything to do with the crime would be *sub judice*, so she would be prevented from speaking to you by law.)

You ring Mrs Jones and she says: 'I've nothing to say to you.'

Try being honest, but regretful: 'Look, I don't like bothering you on this, especially as you had all that trouble of having to go to court. But all I'm writing is a feature on crimes of passion in Yorkshire during the last two decades. Just a pretty ordinary piece – and there are lots of other cases mentioned.

'I know your name, and writing about this case, it's unavoidable that I say you live beneath the couple and heard them rowing. If you'd just answer a couple of my questions I can take down your answers exactly as you say them and at least you'll know that what's printed will be your own accurate version.'

Never threaten people – appeal to sweet reason. (Anyway, it's a punishable offence.) Hint that perhaps readers will think she is telling an untruth unless you can categorically write 'Mrs Jones said . . .' using her very own words.

DIFFICULT NAMES

So you're on the phone – fervently hoping you're going to be able to persuade your potential interviewee to meet you.

With our increasing involvement in Europe, the regular exchange of academics at the world's universities and global tours of performing artists, the person you want to interview may well have a foreign name that's difficult to spell and pronounce. There are plenty of British names in this category too.

People's feelings are hurt if you misspell or mispronounce their names. You know this if it's happened to you, and it's difficult to explain why. But subconsciously our names are extremely important to us (which is why there's always a ceremony for a baby's name-giving).

It's an irritant to your interviewee if you:

1 Spell their name incorrectly in the piece you write.
2 Pronounce their name with the stress in the wrong place or garble it in some other way. So, at the interview, they're not as kindly receptive to your questions as you'd like them to be.

The tip is to get it right on your first contact – the phone call to arrange the interview.

Ask them Make a point of asking them how to *spell* their name, and WRITE IT DOWN. Apart from foreign names there are dozens of British names that have similar sounds but different spellings eg Brown/Browne, Paterson/Pattison, Pierce/Pearce, Sean/Shawn, Steven/Stephen, Jane/Jayne etc.

Also ask how their name is PRONOUNCED – and as they tell you WRITE IT DOWN PHONETICALLY and repeat it after them. For instance, the English name Crichton would be Cry-ton, the French Monet would be Mon-ay, the Chinese Que would be Shoo.

When you've put down the phone, repeat it to yourself phonetically several times whilst looking at the actual spelling. This will get your brain used to the idea so your tongue won't pronounce what your eyes see, if you get my meaning. Then you'll be able to greet your interviewee with 'Hello, Mr Smyth' (which is the way he wants it, even though he spells it Smith), or 'Hello, Ms Sinjen' (which is the way St John is pronounced).

And don't be scared of foreign names. Yes, many of them aren't pronounced the way an English person would, but that's no reason to take a terrified look at the name, see it as merely a jumble of letters, and make an ass of yourself by blurting out some unintelligible gobbledegook.

All you have to do is ASK how it should be pronounced, then write it down phonetically. This is how radio and television announcers handle it. Then you can cope if you have to interview the President of the Serbian government, Mr Slobodan Milosevic, and greet him with: 'Hello, Mr Swobadan Meeloshevich.'

Example

During the phone call what you actually say is:

'May I speak to Mr Sidebottom, please?'

'You mean Mr Siddy-bothomay.'

'Oh sorry, did I get it wrong – could you tell me how it's spelt, please?'

'S.I.D.E.B.O.T.T.O.M.'

'Right – got that. And you pronounce it Siddy-bothomay?'

'Yes.'

'Thanks. Now Mr Siddy-bothomay, first, is it a convenient time for you to speak, please, you're not in the middle of a meal or anything?'

CONFIRM IT

One last vital point – immediately after you've put down the phone, always confirm the appointment in writing. Then you won't arrive and find they've gone out because they forgot you were coming.

It's also a help to both of you in that you repeat in the letter the main theme of your write-up. They then have time to think of the best answers.

EXERCISE

Without re-reading this chapter:

1 List the five items you should have by your side when you pick up the phone.
2 Write out a 'script' to make an appointment with a particular specialist. List in order all the points you should cover, starting with Smile Down the Phone.

CHAPTER 9

To Make It All Right on the Night

- Rehearse
- Fear factor
- Guinea pigs
- Writers' Club
- Practice project – Profile
- Practice project – Feature
- Interviewing criteria
- Criteria for write-ups
- Impromptu interviews
- N.V.Q.
- Press Complaints Commission's Code of Practice
- Exercise.

To DO A PROFESSIONAL JOB of the interview there are five main preparation stages before you actually meet your interviewee – Research, Arrange Appointment, Compile List of Questions, Check Equipment and – REHEARSE.

Anything that's rehearsed has more chance of being 'all right on the night'. No, you can't rehearse the actual interviews you will carry out. But you can act out the TECHNIQUE of interviewing. An Olympic athlete cannot run the actual race until the Games are held; but he sure gets in a great deal of practise beforehand.

Interviewing techniques CAN be learnt from a book, but it's 200 per cent more valuable to get in additional 'hands on' experience before you meet your first real live interviewee.

FEAR FACTOR

Yes, I know how scared you are – but the more you do interviews the less terrifying it gets.

I think one has to accept that a certain amount of dread always accompanies challenge and risk – it's the normal and natural fear of a first-time experience. Nobody is immune from this. So, yes, you feel terrified – well, go ahead and do it anyway. The anxiety won't go away.

It's a bit like going on a long journey – you have to pack a large suitcase with all that you'll need. The suitcase is a pain, you'd travel better without it, but it isn't going to walk by itself. So you hump it with you – and still successfully complete your journey.

The more familiar a situation, the less you fear it. The way to become familiar with a SUCCESSFUL interview is to learn the techniques and practise them as often as you can. That will give you confidence – which is the best antidote to fear. Plain hope and enthusiasm will take you only so far.

It's part of learning to be assertive – NOT aggressive. Professional journalists are assertive and tenacious. You can't have a shy journalist. Many of us – including me – are naturally shy, but we have to learn to role-play – something we turn on just to do the job.

A VALUABLE TIP: you can always take a course in assertiveness – many, many people do this now the job market is so competitive.

There are many assertiveness courses on offer which last a day, a weekend, a week or several months. Check your local Adult Education Centre. You can also send for *Time to Learn*, the directory of courses on hundreds of subjects. The address is: The National Institute of Adult Continuing Education (England and Wales), 19b De Montford Street, Leicester LE1 7GE. (See also Chapter 13.)

GUINEA PIGS

On the courses I teach, students interview each other. As you are a reader I can't offer you this sort of help. But I will show you how to set up self-help rehearsals.

What you need are guinea pigs.

It's not a good idea to use family or close friends. You already know a great deal about them, so that kills the 'discovery' aspect of interviewing. And it's almost impossible not to collapse in a heap of guffaws and giggles because you know each other so well.

Two alternatives are:

(a) people you know only slightly;
(b) members of a Writers' Club.

In the first category you could ask the man who runs the newsagents where you buy your daily paper, your hairdresser, or your squash coach. Or someone at work – the personnel officer, tea lady or shop steward.

Take them into your confidence. Tell them you're training to be a journalist and you have a project to do. Ask them if they'd be kind enough to let you meet them when they're not rushed off their feet, and interview them for ten to thirty minutes.

Many people will be quite interested in the novelty of the idea and their altruism will do the rest. You'll get far more co-operation than my cousin who, when he was studying to be a doctor, kept asking people if they'd mind if he took out their appendix just for a bit of practise!

You explain that nobody will see the write-up but them – you're not going to send it to a newspaper. Yes, letting them see what you've written is part of the exercise. This is so you can discover whether or not you were accurate in quoting them.

WRITERS' CLUB

You should also be able to find guinea pigs in Writers' Clubs. And they will be of more value because they should be able to give you pertinent feedback. They should also be capable of discussing points such as the marketability, style and pace of your write-up.

Your local Reference Library might have a copy of the directory of writers' clubs compiled by Jill Dick.

If there isn't a Writers' Club near you, why don't you start one?

Put a classified ad in your local newspaper and a small, hand-made poster in your local library suggesting that any potential and actual writers meet at your place on alternate Friday evenings, say.

There are a number of other advantages in joining/starting a Writers' Club. Buying paper, ribbons, discs and other stationery is always cheaper in bulk.

While you talk shop you can compare working methods.

PRACTICE PROJECT – PROFILE

You're going to interview your guinea pig for ten minutes (time it), and write a 250-word profile on them.

Before you interview them ask them:

(a) name;
(b) where they were born;
(c) job;
(d) hobbies.

You want single-word answers, nothing more.

Research   With this basic information (the equivalent to what you'd know about a Big Name), you start doing your research. If they said they were born in Galway, then look up books on the place. If they say they are a quality control officer, get hold of a career book on that. And I don't need to point out how to research hobbies – just be sure you know the difference between abseiling and hang gliding, or crocheting and macramé.

Questions – C.Q.R.   You've done the research. Now work out a C.Q.R. graph to help you compile a list of questions (see Chapter 2).

Questions – The List   Now call on the journalist's six friends to organise you. You already know the Who, Where and What (above). At the interview you aim to discover the When, Why and How.

Find a piece of blank A4 size paper. On the left list the trigger words, WHO, WHAT, WHERE, WHEN, WHY, HOW.

Those six questions apply over and over again in interviewing – they're the six facts you need about most situations. Start with the person's job – then when you've asked those six questions about that, start all over again on things they do in their leisure time using questions starting with WHO, WHAT, WHERE, WHEN, WHY, HOW.

The way it helps you is this – let's first find out about their job – WHO: you put the name of the company they work for, CHECKING SPELLING is correct. WHAT job do you do? WHERE are you based? WHEN did you start the job (to discover how long they've been doing it). WHY become a blacksmith or a computer programmer? HOW did you become this – training you took? By the time you've got those basics you start expanding to ask what they like/dislike about the job – what it actually entails, what does it pay? and anything else you think of.

When you've exhausted all those, go on to what your subject does in her/his out-of-job hours AND USE THAT SEQUENCE of who, what, where, when, why, how again. WHAT do you do to relax? WHERE do you do it (alone, at a Sports Club?) WHEN (how often)? WHY, what motivated your interest? HOW – did you go to evening classes? learn on holiday? Then expand. Those six trigger words are merely to help you get the basics. Ask them in any order you like.

A profile concentrates on the WHOLE PERSON, not, repeat NOT, just their job. Aim at rounded pieces on the entire person – their PERSONALITY, general lifestyle, aspirations.

When interviewing you're aiming at discovering WHAT MAKES THIS PERSON DIFFERENT? Find out what your subject does or thinks that's unusual – everyone's an individual. The creative part of questioning is discovering what it is.

This practice project (or these, as I hope you'll do a number of rehearsal interviews), is a good opportunity to test out your new recording machine.

If you can persuade your 'guinea pig' to return for another interview, make the next one different. Do something specific rather than their whole life, such as a holiday they went on, a stay in hospital or some interesting after-work activity. And, of course, write it up afterwards.

PRACTICE PROJECT – FEATURE

When you've done a few straightforward profiles, give yourself more of a challenge by interviewing a few people for a feature – you choose the topic. And always go into the interviews with this clear objective noted down in outline. This is to stop you wasting time digressing, or forgetting which 'angle' is the focus of the piece.

For your subject you might have decided on 'women priests', and the angle – 'what are the advantages and disadvantages?'

So you interview a laboratory assistant, say. Don't go wandering too far into how many hours she spends at her bench or what projects she's working on as these would be questions you'd ask for a PROFILE. You're now doing a FEATURE. So instead of asking the laboratory assistant about her own lifestyle, you'd be delving for her opinions on women priests.

One of my private students, Paul, made this mistake. The project was a news story (not a profile), and for the interview I had brought in Margaret, who had raised £670 for the British Heart Foundation. She got people to sponsor her bike ride from London to Brighton.

The interview started by Paul asking Margaret what she did. She told him she was the Sister in the casualty department of a big hospital. Paul was naturally fascinated by this and asked all sorts of interesting questions like: 'What cases did you have in last week?' 'Do you have people who have been attacked?' 'Do many die?' – the sorts of questions anyone would ask.

But Paul wasn't 'anyone'. He was a trainee journalist interviewing for details about a bicycle ride that raised money for charity.

There was a time limit on the interview, and when that was up Paul didn't have half the information he needed to write the news story.

So when you've decided on your angle, glue it into your brain and don't let extraneous topics deter you.

INTERVIEWING CRITERIA

If you can practise as a group of three or more you can have one person watching and assessing the performance as follows (you could make several photocopies of this questionnaire and use one for each interview):

Did the interviewer	Yes	No
1 Put interviewee at ease, pleasantly and effectively?		
2 Look pleasant and have good eye contact?		
3 Check the spelling of interviewee's name?		
4 CONTROL the interview?		
5 Talk too much?		
6 Ask 'open-ended' questions? (i.e. Who, What, Where, Why, When, How)		
7 Ask questions that led out of one another logically, and didn't dart about haphazardly?		
8 Explore topic sufficiently and not still leave avenues unexplored?		
9 Ask questions that developed out of answers given because s/he was effectively listening to the answers?		
10 Use the word 'why?' frequently?		
11 Ask about future plans?		

CRITERIA FOR WRITE-UPS

Another advantage of joining a Writers' Club is that you'll have people to ask for an objective criticism of the pieces you write. Showing your write-ups to your Mum or other half seldom gets an unbiased crit.

This is what you want to know:

1 Does the first sentence have enough impact to TEMPT THE READER TO READ ON?

2 Does the writer use plenty of quotes? (The more the better. But remember, you can only put into quotes words that were actually said by the interviewee, or they agreed to when the interviewer asked: 'Would you say that . . . ?')

3 Is it free of clichés?

4 Is it free of repetition?

5 Are the sentences short, not more than 27 words?

6 Does it have a significant ending (perhaps about future plans) or does it merely stop in mid-air?

7 Ask the subject if s/he did in fact say what you put in quotes.

NB: When writing profiles for a specific publication, there's the additional criteria of:

8 Writing in the 'house style';

9 Writing strictly to length;

10 Format – Q&A or Feature.

IMPROMPTU INTERVIEWS

By the way, don't think these ten-minute, practice interviews are nothing like the real thing. The need for a short, impromptu interview can strike at any time. You'll be introduced to someone – in a pub, say, or at a party – and realise that her speciality or experience would make a super feature or profile. BUT – she's leaving the country in the next half an hour. So you ASK HER PERMISSION TO INTERVIEW HER ON THE SPOT – and there's your ten-minute interview.

What you always fall back on to start with are the newspaper reporter's six essential questions – WHO, WHAT, WHERE, WHY, WHEN, HOW.

N.V.Q.

As beginners, it might help you to know what a staff journalist is expected to deal with when researching features. This will give you something to aim at.

Should you want to work on a newspaper, you will probably get on-the-job assessment under the National Vocational Qualification scheme run by the Royal Society of Arts. In the case of research for the treatment of features, these are the Performance Criteria (i.e. what you're expected to know and be able to do):

1   Appropriate information sources are consulted and relevant information is extracted.
2   Contradictions in information are resolved where possible, if necessary by consulting original sources.
3   Research data are used as required in progressing assignments.
4   Legal implications of research data are recognised and the appropriate action taken.

Range covered: internal and external libraries, cuttings libraries, cuttings services, picture libraries, photographers and illustrators, electronic information sources.

And on carrying out the actual interview the Performance Criteria are:

1   The interview technique adopted is appropriate for the needs of the assignment and the circumstances of the interview, and elicits the optimum amount of information.
2   Relevant interview leads are followed up as required.
3   Accurate and relevant note is taken, including verbatim note of appropriate quotes (you need shorthand).
4   Arrangements are made for possible future contacts with interviewees.

5   Relevant information sources are sought from interviewees.
6   Discrepancies and inconsistencies in information are resolved where possible.
7   Legal and ethical implications of activities are recognised and appropriate action taken.
    Range covered:
Interviews: face-to-face and telephone, pre-arranged and impromptu, fact and opinion, positive and hostile.

Interview technique: establishing of rapport, pace, use of closed and open questions, unambiguous questioning, checking and confirming information, giving information.

CODE OF PRACTICE

Another aspect of the profession which will be of value to aspiring journalists is to know the Code of Practice of the Press Complaints Commission (ex-Press Council).

Press Complaints Commission

Code of Practice

All members of the Press have a duty to maintain the highest professional and ethical standards.
In doing so, they should have regard to the provisions of this code of practice and to safeguarding the public's right to know.

Editors are responsible for the actions of journalists employed by their publications. They should also satisfy themselves as far as possible that material accepted from non-staff members was obtained in accordance with this code.

While recognising that this involves a substantial element of self-restraint by editors and journalists, it is designed to be acceptable in the context of a system of self-regulation. The code applies in the spirit as well as in the letter.

Accuracy

1. Newspapers and periodicals should take care not to publish inaccurate, misleading or distorted material.

2. Whenever it is recognised that a significant inaccuracy, misleading statement or distorted report has been published, it should be corrected promptly and with due prominence.

3. An apology should be published whenever appropriate.

4. A newspaper or periodical should always report fairly and accurately the outcome of an action for defamation to which it has been a party.

Opportunity to reply

A fair opportunity for reply to inaccuracies should be given to individuals or organisations when reasonably called for.

Comment, conjecture and fact

Newspapers, whilst free to be partisan, should distinguish clearly between comment, conjecture and fact.

Privacy

Intrusions and inquiries into an individual's private life without his or her consent are not generally acceptable and publication can only be justified when in the public interest. This would include:

a. Detecting or exposing crime or serious misdemeanour.

b. Detecting or exposing seriously anti-social conduct.

c. Protecting public health and safety.

d. Preventing the public from being misled by some statement or action of that individual.

Hospitals

1. Journalists or photographers making inquiries at hospitals or similar institutions should identify themselves to a responsible official and obtain permission before entering non-public areas.

2. The restrictions on intruding into privacy are particularly relevant to inquiries about individuals in hospitals or similar institutions.

Misrepresentation

1. Journalists should not generally obtain or seek to obtain information or pictures through misrepresentation or subterfuge.

2. Unless in the public interest, documents or photographs should be removed only with express consent of the owner.

3. Subterfuge can be justified only in the public interest and only when material cannot be obtained by any other means.

In all these clauses the public interest includes:

a. Detecting or exposing crime or serious misdemeanor.

b. Detecting or exposing anti-social conduct.

c. Protecting public health or safety.

d. Preventing the public being misled by some statement or action of an individual or organisation.

Harassment

1. Journalists should neither obtain nor seek to obtain information or pictures through intimidation.

2. Unless their inquiries are in the public interest, journalists should not photograph individuals or private property without their consent; should not persist in telephoning or questioning individuals after having been asked to leave and should not follow them. The public interest would include:

a. Detecting or exposing crime or serious misdemeanour.

b. Detecting or exposing anti-social conduct.

c. Protecting public health and safety.

d. Preventing the public from being misled by some statement or action of that individual or organisation.

Payment for articles

1. Payments or offers of payment for stories, pictures or information should not be made to witnesses or potential witnesses in current criminal proceedings or to people engaged in crime or to their associates except where the material concerned ought to be published in the public interest and the payment is necessary for this to be done.

The public interest will include:

a. Detecting or exposing crime or serious misdemeanour,

b. Detecting or exposing anti-social conduct,

c. Protecting public health and safety,

d. Preventing the public from being misled by some statement or action of that individual or organisation.

2. 'Associates' including family, friends, neighbours and colleagues.

3. Payments should not be made either directly or indirectly through agents.

Intrusion into grief or shock

In cases involving personal grief or shock, inquiries should be carried out and approaches made with sympathy and discretion.

Innocent relatives and friends

The Press should generally avoid identifying relatives or friends of persons convicted or accused of crime unless the reference to them is necessary for the full, fair and accurate reporting of the crime or legal proceedings.

Interviewing or photographing children

1. Journalists should not normally interview or photograph children under the age of 16 on subjects involving the personal welfare of the child, in the absence of or without the consent of a parent or other adult who is responsible for the children.

2. Children should not be approached or photographed while at school without the permission of the school authorities.

Children in sex cases

The Press should not, even where the law does not prohibit it, identify children under the age of 16 who are involved in cases concerning sexual offences, whether as victims, or as witnesses or defendants.

Victims of crime

The Press should not identify victims of sexual assault or

publish material likely to contribute to such identification unless, by law, they are free to do so.

Discrimination

1. The Press should avoid prejudicial or pejorative reference to a person's race, colour, religion, sex or sexual orientation or to any physical or mental illness or handicap.

2. It should avoid publishing details of a person's race, colour, religion, sex or sexual orientation, unless these are directly relevant to the story.

Financial journalism

1. Even where the law does not prohibit it, journalists should not use for their own profit financial information they receive in advance of its general publication, nor should they pass such information to others.

2. They should not write about shares or securities in whose performance they know that they or their close families have a significant financial interest, without disclosing the interest to the editor or financial editor.

3. They should not buy or sell, either directly or through nominees or agents, shares or securities about which they have written recently or about which they intend to write in the near future.

Confidential sources

Journalists have a moral obligation to protect confidential sources of information.

EXERCISE

The exercise for this chapter is to practise interviewing. But before you do, read up to Chapter 15 as there's still a great deal more to learn.

CHAPTER 10

Planning Questions

- Don't run out
- Don't show them
- Be incisive
- Have a theme
- Chronology
- Several markets
- Make the most of it
- Security blanket
- Biography
- Exercise.

A MAJOR NIGHTMARE for interviewers is to run out of questions. Always go into an interview with more prepared questions than you know you can ask in the time agreed. You'd be surprised how many times it runs over time. Even when your subject has implicitly stated that he won't answer questions on X and Z, once you've got him relaxed and the dialogue rolling, he'll often change his mind.

DON'T SHOW THEM

One of my students asked me whether or not you should show your interviewee your questions beforehand. I'm strongly against this because you will ruin the spontaneity of their answers. And it's spontaneity which gives 'life' to their comments – and to your write-up. Remember, you have to SELL it.

If they ask (and only if they do), the best riposte is: 'Sorry, it isn't journalistic policy, but to reassure you, let me tell you that all I'm going to ask is . . . general questions about your childhood, schooldays, first job, marriage – that sort of stuff', or '. . . general questions about your job and how you designed the spaceship/computer game/Christmas card.'

That word 'general' is reassuring to them – it doesn't sound as though you're going to probe.

BE INCISIVE

At the interview you will ask two types of questions:

1   those derived from research you've done beforehand;
2   those that develop from the answers your subject gives you.

With the questions prepared beforehand you have the opportunity to be very incisive. Before the event you are cool-headed and able to focus entirely on the piece you're finally going to write. Face-to-face with your subject you have to concentrate on listening to their answers and formulating questions from those. So prepare a good, long list of questions thrown up by research.

Your C.Q.R. graph is invaluable at the research stage. It creates questions for which you do and do not have answers. The interview is the opportunity to plug the gaps in your knowledge.

Example 1

For a profile you are going to interview a famous horror fiction writer. Among other queries on your C.Q.R. you ask yourself: 'What specifically is his definition of horror?' 'Why, apart from making money, does he write horror instead of, say, children's books or crime?' Those are gaps in your knowledge, so those are the questions you list to ask.

Example 2

For a Day-in-the-life-of feature you are to interview a British woman doctor who works in famine-torn Somalia. 'How does she cope with the unhygienic conditions and the perpetual flies?' 'Why doesn't she prefer a nice safe NHS hospital in Milton Keynes?' 'Does she have any social life at all?' 'If so, exactly what is it?' More gaps equal more questions.

Be professionally objective. You will sell it only if you get a really ORIGINAL piece from the interview. Yes, you sometimes see rather run-of-the-mill stuff published, but that is written by established journalists – you're only on the first rung of the ladder and unknown to any editor. So plan out beforehand the outline of your write-up to make a fascinating read.

The C.Q.R. will start with the ordinary, banal: 'Where were you born/schooled/first worked catechism', but your journalistic curiosity should then delve into areas that will give your write-up that extra sparkle necessary to tempt an editor to buy it.

Example

A professional journalist tries to focus on profound discoveries that reveal the interviewee's exclusive personality, actions, philosophy, method of tackling problems, or lifestyle,

Harry Hunk's agent gives a press reception in London. He's here to promote his latest film *Blood and Guts*. You're told that, as with all the other journalists there, you have 30 minutes with him. You guess all the other journalists will be concentrating on his film: 'Did he do any of the fights or was it all stunt men?' 'Did he hurt the female lead when the script called for him to sock her?' – that sort of thing.

You decide that yes, you'll ask those sorts of questions but make them very short. You've an idea for a really telling interview.

The headlines in yesterday's newspapers were shouting about teenage hooliganism in schools. You are going to devote most of your 30 minutes to hooliganism. Here's an opportunity to turn in a TOPICAL piece because it's linked with what's currently in the news.

'Mr Hunk, *Blood and Guts* is a very violent film. Although there were a couple of places where there was an element of tongue-in-cheek, overall it was blatantly bloodthirsty. Is the film's message "Real Men are violent"?' '*Blood and Guts* features several teenagers; would you say it encouraged or discouraged hooliganism?' And so on.

The answers to these questions could be mere grunts if Harry Hunk has muscles between his ears as well as everywhere else. On the other hand, he may be in the typecast spiral and unhappy that his intelligence is underestimated. He may welcome an opportunity to sound off about the unfortunate effect screen violence possibly has on young, impressionable males. If so, there you have a far more saleable profile than you would have had if you merely stuck to the film.

HAVE A THEME

When doing a profile don't let either the questions or the finished write-up wander all over the place. Try and plot a theme, a premise, and whatever questions you ask, keep returning to that theme so you 'tell a story'.

Example You interview Samantha Saga whose novel *Feud* has been in the Bestseller List for ten weeks running. The details you received from her publisher told you, among other things, that she'd been with the Inland Revenue for 25 years. You want your theme to be 'How an Income Tax Inspector ends up as a novelist'.

You ask why writing wasn't her first job. Her reply will possibly be don't know, and anyway her parents pushed her towards a good, steady job. Did it take long to become a Tax Inspector? Yes, years. Were you thinking about writing all that time? Yes, always at back of my mind, in fact I took a writing course at evening classes and wrote short stories.

Why leave tax job after a quarter of a century? I'd had enough, no job satisfaction. Did you ever think of making writing a career? Yes, but hadn't the confidence. So when I first left the Inland Revenue I freelanced as a marketing consultant specialising in tax. Ah, freelancing, your first step towards working in isolation as a writer does? Yes, and at the back of my mind also had an idea for a novel which I worked on between clients.

Was the novel published, Ms Saga? No, but I learnt a great deal. I took it to writing seminars and workshops, all a learning process. Sounds all work and no play? Actually no, decided to spice up life by learning gliding. I wrote a feature about it, my first acceptance, boosted my confidence.

What else do you do in your spare time? Became secretary of a Rape Support Group. My eyes were opened to the appalling number of rapes and other forms of violence. So that's where you got your plot for *Feud*? Yes, and I wanted to give it an interesting background so instead of taking my usual holiday in Greece, I went to Nepal.

What about future novels? I've just finished a sequel to *Feud* and am part way through another; it's a trilogy. All basically about women victims of violence, but each book is set in a different country. No.2 is set in Thailand, No.3 in Java. Why choose these countries? I developed an interest in them from beautiful postage stamps, I'm a keen philatelist . . . and so on.

Do you see how this developed? Samantha Saga's life is many faceted, but the interviewer tried to find the relevance of these aspects to WRITING wherever possible. The result is a 'running story' on the theme of her writing, rather than a collection of unrelated bits. When interviewing you wouldn't necessarily be asking questions in this chronological order, but you WOULD be finding out the relevance (if any) of each event to your basic angle, i.e. that she's now an established author. Hence, you need to be remembering your theme throughout the interview so you can weave the profile into a story.

CHRONOLOGY

It's a good idea when listing questions to take to the interview to write them down chronologically – schooldays, teenage, first romance, first marriage, first baby etc. This makes it much easier for you to transcribe.

This doesn't mean, of course, that you're necessarily going to write the piece chronologically. In fact, it's better not to as this would be predictable and perhaps a trifle boring. It would certainly be unoriginal.

SEVERAL MARKETS

And when preparing your questions do remember to plan a few specifically for EACH MARKET YOU CAN SELL TO.

Example

The subject is Deborah Drama – she's the star of the about-to-be-released film *Dark Attraction*. The editor is expecting a profile on her angled at the new film. Additionally, you've got the editor of another publication interested in another angle – her views on 'the problems of having a celeb for a parent'. Your list of questions has to be carefully calculated to gather information for both specific goals.

And be flexible when you get in there. What frequently happens is your subject will gallop off down a verbal avenue that will lead to some gems of revelation on something quite different. These will be treasures that could never have occurred to you while you were doing your C.Q.R. Great! You're in luck.

You could include them alongside the star's views on celeb parents. Or, if the new details just won't fit into the piece you're writing, perhaps they have enough substance to stand on their own. Then you can make them the focus of yet another write-up. You can sell it to a different publication.

After you've thoroughly explored the unexpected points Deborah Drama revealed, your list helps you steer your subject back to the path you want her to take, to questions on *Dark Attraction* and on parenting.

The series of questions you worked out is a map to guide you so you can steer the interview towards the destinations (angles) you originally interested editors in.

Remember, editors aren't looking for stream-of-consciousness pieces from unknowns.

MAKE THE MOST OF IT

Your research also told you that Deborah Drama lives in a designer-decorated mansion with a designer-landscaped garden, so you prepared questions to ask on that too. And when you've been talking for a good hour, she is really starting to reveal, she tells you about the cot death of her second baby.

So you get four write-ups from that one interview:

1 Preview of *Dark Attraction* – could be for *Daily Mail*;
2 Problems of having a celeb for a parent – *Guardian* or a women's glossy monthly magazine;
3 Deborah Drama's fabulous mansion – *House and Garden*;
4 The star's tragic loss of her baby – *Best* or *Bella*.

Example Let's take Edward Epic:

1 The editor of *Esquire* is interested in your main profile on his latest book.
2 As Mr Epic lives in a rather delightful 13th-century weaver's house, you've also got an eye on *Ideal Home* for another profile. For this piece you'll need answers to questions on the house itself and its surrounding acres.
3 Let's say our Edward has a passion for Siamese cats and owns three. *Cat World* might well take a profile on him and his pets.
4 And you discover he owns and sails a nice little line in yachts. So again, you plan questions about this side of his life with an eye on *Yachting World*.

This is getting as much mileage as you can from one interview. So you need constant market research sessions in a large newsagents plus a list of questions pre-planned for each title.

SECURITY BLANKET

Another tangible use for that list of questions – it's a great comfort if you confront an interviewee who gives you problems. Just because you come up with a good question doesn't mean you'll get a good answer, or one of any decent length.

I remember two very relevant instances.

I had two appointments in the same week. They were both with household name thespians, one appearing at the Haymarket and the other at the Old Vic.

I prepared two very similar lists of questions for them both. As it takes roughly 20 minutes to 'warm up' your subject, I carefully scheduled for about halfway through the session the question: 'Who, if anyone, has had a significant effect on your career?'

The male actor at the Haymarket answered: 'Nobody.' So that took up two seconds and I moved on to the next question.

The actress at the Old Vic answered after a few moments' thought: 'Han Suyin, the writer, scholar and surgeon. Her words have quite profoundly affected not only my career but my entire life.' And she went on for 15 minutes to describe how she'd read Han Suyin's five-book autobiography plus her autobiographical novels. The author's thoughts as a woman intellectual in post-revolution China had motivated the actress to change many of her opinions and some of her lifestyle. Additionally, they had a significant affect on her approach to some of the parts she played on stage.

So there you have two entirely different reactions to the same question. The actor's reply, like many he gave me, was curt in the extreme. So if I'd gone in with only half a dozen questions I'd soon have run out of steam.

The actress was so deeply passionate about a person she admired profoundly, I was in danger of being overcome by her fervour and trapped into letting her talk about Han Suyin for the rest of the interview. But after I'd got a couple of good quotes about Han Suyin, I needed to remind myself of other topics I wanted covered. So I was able to refer to the tangible list of questions clutched firmly in my hot little hand.

Remember the interviewer is always sailing in unknown waters. An inflatable canoe (heavily disguised as a long list of extra questions, most hooked to a theme) is a good contingency plan.

BIOGRAPHY

By the way, don't be afraid of thinking BIG. It could be that
your interviewee turns out to have had a particularly event-
packed life, also that you and s/he get on very well together.
In the future you could think of writing their biography. Many
publishers are on the lookout for well-written biographies of
celebrities.

EXERCISE

List five questions to ask Harry Hunk on violence that I
haven't already mentioned.

CHAPTER 11

More on Planning Questions: Open-ended Ones and Others

- WWWWWH
- Trigger words
- Predictable answers
- Auto-suggestion
- Avoid multiples
- Be specific

- Clichés
- Communicate
- Understand the answers
- Asking is OK
- Original questions
- Exercise.

WWWWWH

WHATEVER the interview, you need never be at a loss for questions to ask if you use Who, What, Where, When, Why and How.

The great advantage of using this formula as often as you can is that they will all be open-ended questions. This means they can't be answered with a simple 'yes' or 'no'.

'Yes' and 'No' replies make pretty boring reading, and you're not into sending your reader to sleep, but entertaining them. So, the answers you want aren't simple affirmation or denial – what an editor needs is opinion, anecdote and information.

Example You're interviewing a soccer star. You ask: 'Do you have to have the killer instinct to play for the World Cup?'

He can only answer 'Yes' or 'No'. But if you had started the question with one of the WWWWWH words he would have given a much more expansive reply.

'What qualities, apart from the killer instinct, do you need to be in the World Cup team?' He would agree about the need for killer instinct (or disagree), but he'd also list other skills/techniques such as 'precision timing and 200 per cent fitness'.

Never forget that YOU have to control the interview, YOU have to steer the interviewee towards giving answers that will make your write-up sell. And asking open-ended questions is one of the major techniques of the professional journalist. Yes, it takes practice, but there's only six words to glue into your brain. Try it out when in conversation with friends.

Rescue

If you find at the interview that you're asking 'closed' questions, your follow-up should always be: 'Why?' Try and glue that into your brain too. Almost every 'Yes' and 'No' can be chased by a 'Why?'

TRIGGER WORDS

You don't list your questions verbatim – that would take too long to read. You use trigger words.

Example   You're interviewing a leading Press photographer. Your list looks something like this:

1 Photos – where?
2 Last one – what?
3 Where?
4 When?
5 Who there?
6 Why?
7 How go?

But what you actually asked was:

1   *Question* – Where do you go to take photos?
    Answer Buckingham Palace, Trades Unions conferences,
    top political meetings.
2   *Q* Let's take the Unions first – what was the last
    conference?
3   *Q* Where was it held?
4   *Q* When?
5   *Q* Who was there – what big names?
6   *Q* Why was it held – what was on the agenda?
7   *Q* How did it go – were the main points resolved?
8   *Q* And now the Palace. What was going on the last time
    you were there – investitures?
9   *Q* When was it?
10 *Q* Who invested the honours – the Queen or Queen
    Mum?
11 *Q* Who received what? Who were the big names?

And so on.

PREDICTABLE ANSWERS

Before you list a question, think of what the reply could be. If
you really analyse it, the old chestnut 'How does it feel?' is
pretty innocuous in that you can often predict the answer.

'How does it feel to be world champion?' – Well they're
hardly going to say 'awful', are they? And the same with any
achievement a person has made.

On the other hand if they've just suffered something tragic:
'How does it feel to have AIDS?' won't get the answer: 'Great.'

The questions need to be more subtle.

'When you heard you'd been left £2 million by your uncle,
did you rush out and celebrate?' followed by: 'What did you
do, get drunk, book a holiday?' or 'OK, no celebration. What
was the first thing you did with the money?'

And for a tragedy: 'When you learned your lover had been
sentenced to life imprisonment, what was your first thought
about your relationship? After all, it's a bit unrealistic to expect
you to remain faithful for 15 years.'

Interviewing is the CREATIVE part of the discovery process. Getting information from book research isn't – it's merely copying.

AUTO-SUGGESTION

The way in which you question – the actual words you use – is extremely important because you could bias your interviewee's thinking.

Example   the topic is 'The queen should/should not pay income tax.'

In a borough in south-east England two separate house-to-house surveys were carried out. The monitors were both in the same area and took alternate streets.

QUESTION 'A': If the queen paid income tax there'd be enough money to build 40 new schools. Should she or should she not pay? 87 per cent said she should.

QUESTION 'B': A number of people have been discussing whether or not the queen should pay income tax. Do you agree or disagree? 54 per cent said she should.

AVOID MULTIPLES

Don't confuse your subject by asking multiple questions. Picture your subject's reaction after you've asked: 'What made you decide on catering for a career – was you mother a good cook – where did you go for training and do you find catering creative?'

Ask one at a time.

BE SPECIFIC

Try not to make your questions too general. It helps your subject give a rational answer if they can focus on one particular point. For instance, don't ask: 'What is the meaning of life?' or 'What would solve all the world's problems?' All you're going to get in most cases is waffle.

Taking the last one – if you want an answer you can quote, be specific about WHICH problem, also about WHICH country. Tackle them one by one. Ask: 'Looking at Somalia and other places stricken by drought, what do you think can be done about the famine?'

CLICHÉS

If I suggested you avoid cliché questions altogether that would be unrealistic. Old chestnuts such as: 'Where were you born? Where did you go to school?' and that ilk are recognised groundwork.

But to carry on with banal questions throughout the interview is uncreative and unprofessional (also unsaleable!). What you don't want are cliché ANSWERS.

It happens sometimes with people who have been interviewed too often, like celebs. They become blasé and spin out the same old answers to every journalist.

With them you have to be extra creative in working out questions they've not been asked before. This is where thorough research pays off. Hunt out previous profiles on the person you're going to interview so you know what points haven't been covered.

COMMUNICATE

Use language your subject can UNDERSTAND. Don't try to come over all erudite by deliberately using long words or being ambiguous. You're not there to impress but to dig for answers. A journalist is a COMMUNICATOR, so use simple, easily understandable words. If you don't, they will be too shy or embarrassed to ask you to explain, and all you'll get is silence or 'I don't know'.

UNDERSTAND THE ANSWERS

It's very unprofessional to have to phone your interviewee afterwards to ask what they meant when they said XXX. You must be THINKING while you're at the interview. Don't just rely on your dictating machine to record the answer which 'wasn't all that clear, but you'll worry about that later'.

Example   you could be talking to a police surgeon after someone was attacked in the street and left unconscious.
Q   Are the victim's injuries superficial or do you think there'll be any lasting damage?
A   Difficult to say at this stage, but I guess there's nothing too serious here. However if the external ophthalmoplegia persists that would give cause for concern.

You only half-heard the last bit – you don't have your tape recorder with you – you scribble it down phonetically intending to look it up in a medical dictionary later.

But did he say ophthalmia or ophthalmoplegia? The first merely means inflammation of the eye. The second, paralysis of one or both eyes. It's imperative you get it right in print. The best strategy is to ASK HIM HOW TO SPELL IT. Never be afraid of appearing ignorant. That's why you're asking questions.

Example   Or you could be interviewing a specialist. You ask: 'Does your eminent colleague Dr Black share your opinions?' The reply is: 'Oh no, she's an ideologist.' Or was that idealist?

You have to be certain because they don't mean the same. The sense of your following question depends on your having understood the last answer. Again, ASK. Repeat the word after your interviewee – 'Ideologist, yes, I see.' If you're wrong, you'll be corrected.

And even if you have the word correct, it could be that you're uncertain of the exact meaning. The way around this is to ask: 'What exactly do YOU mean by ideologist. Can you give me an example of Dr Black's methods?'

Another pitfall, a little knowledge is a dangerous thing. Don't pretend familiarity with your interviewee's speciality unless you're a fellow specialist. Otherwise he will assume you have a working knowledge and won't explain basics. He will also use jargon, and this is usually incomprehensible to an outsider.

ASKING IS OK

Don't be shy to ask questions. Many beginners have a mental bloc that starts in childhood. We're brought up not to ask personal questions – and that's right.

But journalistic interviews are an entirely different situation. The interviewer and interviewee have met for no other reason than that one will question and the other will answer.

In other words, by agreeing to meet you the subject has AGREED to be questioned. Interviewing is an artificial setup where both parties know what to expect and what roles to play.

ORIGINAL QUESTIONS

For original questions to ask, there's no shortage of examples.

Read the hundreds of profiles and features published in newspapers and magazines daily. Analyse the questions asked, note the ones you liked, and use them yourself.

And don't forget to ask the editor. When you originally sell the idea to her, find out if there's anything she would particularly like to know about Gloria Glamour or Harry Hunk. The editor will be pleased to tell you (as long as you have outlined a good, saleable angle of your own already, so it doesn't look as though you're asking her because you haven't a creative thought in your head).

To make your piece unique try and discover something about the director's film, author's book, scientist's survey or athlete's training programme that is unusual. Ask is it the first of its kind? or the largest, smallest, most expensive, produced on a budget, largest team of people employed on it, smallest team, whatever.

Avoid the stereotyped questions. Try these twenty-one:

Who is your role model/hero?
When you were a child were you a leader or a follower?
Who or what taught you something of value that you acted on or benefited by?
What sort of job would you look for if you were made redundant tomorrow?
What do you hate most about your job/husband/wife?
Who was your first date?
Who was the first person you ever loved?
How did you meet your wife/husband?
Who would you like to spend a day with?
If you could go back in time, in what century would you choose to live?
If you won £1 million, what would you buy?
What was your greatest opportunity?
What are the advantages/disadvantages to the public of the job you do?
When was the last time you cried, and why?
How many times have people tried to bribe you?
If you were allowed by law to kill someone, who would it be?
What comes first, friendship or work?
What was your biggest disappointment?
What did you do when you finished the concert/won the prize?
How much do you earn/what were you paid for that film/book?
How would you like to be remembered by the public?

Frankly, what sells is gossip. No, you might not like to admit this but it is part of the craft of journalism. Readers love to know about other people's private lives and thoughts. There are hundreds of interesting little questions to ask without descending to trivial tittle-tattle such as 'What colour are your bedroom curtains?'

EXERCISE

1 Quickly, off the top of your head, think of three unusual questions to ask Gloria Glamour.
2 Write them down.
3 Were they all open-ended?
4 If not, re-write the same questions so they start with one of the WWWWWH words.

CHAPTER 12

Before You Leave Home, Check

- Taking down the words
- Writing implements
- Notebook
- Retrieval of notes
- Shorthand: Impromptu interviews, Methods, Invent your own

- Tape recorders: Survey, Advantages, Disadvantages, What to buy, Batteries/Mains, Tapes
- Keep tapes and notes
- Camera
- Final contingencies
- Exercise.

At LAST, you're nearly ready to leave for the interview. But never go without a thorough check of your equipment – EVEN THOUGH YOU CHECKED IT YESTERDAY.

It's a good idea to write yourself a list, preferably on coloured cardboard, which is more durable than paper and will last. Every time you leave you can tick off the items.

Many of you will say: 'Oh this is a right bore, I won't bother.' And you'll learn the hard way.

When you're actually at the interview, it's a point of no return. Many interviewees' time is precious. So if your dictating machine dies on you or you haven't a pen that will write, they may not be able to give you another appointment in time for your deadline.

It also looks so AMATEUR when the tape snarls up and you haven't another cassette.

TAKING DOWN THE WORDS

Journalism means interviewing people, plus taking notes of lectures, speeches, TV and radio programmes – all the spoken word. Everyone speaks far faster than it is possible to write longhand. A dictating machine/tape recorder AND shorthand are essentials.

WRITING IMPLEMENTS

Pencils break. Fibre-tips, ballpoints and fountain pens run out of ink. Fountain pen nibs are inclined to judder when writing at speed; and with wear, fibre-tips can go soft or splay.

I favour a ballpoint every time – and always take three. Murphy's law decrees that the one you're using will run out of ink just as your subject's saying: 'The last words he uttered were . . .' or 'The person I suspect is . . .'

NOTEBOOK

Buy reporters' notebooks which are about A5 size, have ruled pages and are spiral bound.

It's amazing how many people don't know how to use a notebook. Yes, I mean it. And if you haven't been taught you'll get into an impossible muddle when you want to refer to your notes.

You open the book at the first page, and when that's full you flip over the sheet and start writing on the following page. And so on through the book. You never, never flip over the sheet, then turn the book around so you're writing on the reverse of the page you've just finished.

This can't be done at the speed you must move in an interview. Professionals never interrupt the interviewee and ask them to wait every time they turn a page and turn the book around. It's far faster to rapidly flip over the page and carry on writing on the next page that presents itself.

RETRIEVAL OF NOTES

If you can get into this habit it has two advantages;

1 Speed – as I've just explained;
2 Ease of reference – you know you've chronologically stayed on one side of the page all the way through the book and didn't turn around till you ran out of pages. Then there's no panic when you come to the foot of a page, riffling through trying to discover how many times you turned the book around for the continuing page – or didn't.

Ensure the notebook you take has AT LEAST HALF of its pages still blank. You never know whether the interview will run over time. It's often during the overtime that your subject is likely to reveal all sorts of little gems. This is because, having been talking to you for an hour, they've learned to trust you, and are far more relaxed.

Another point. It's surprising how many people unleash a few more really telling quotes when they see you switch off the tape recorder. You need empty pages to take down this extra revelation.

And another point. A recording machine can break down – there's not a lot can go wrong with a pen and paper.

It helps you think

And yet another point. Even though you're using a tape recorder, YOU STILL TAKE NOTES. There are five ways note-taking helps, even while the machine is recording:

1 Questions occur to you from what your subject is saying. But they may not be convenient to ask at that moment because you don't want to interrupt your interviewee's train of thought. Your note reminds you to ask them later in the interview.
2 You can note down the numbers on the recorder's scale where your subject makes comments on particular topics. You'll be grateful for this later. A one-hour tape can take five hours to transcribe on the typewriter or word processor.

The interviewee will hop about and return to his topic at different points in the interview. When you're writing your piece you need to know where on the tape are all the comments on child molesting, say, or how she works out her best-seller plots.

3 Note your doubts and suspicions. By their body language and tone of voice, in places you may suspect they are uncertain of their facts, are lying or are being cagey. Make a note to check it out afterwards.

4 As they talk you will notice interesting facets which will capture the 'spirit' of your subject, his genuine persona, and give 'human flavour' to your write-up. I mean points about their attire (designer fashion, ethnic, kinky, scruffy); mannerisms (elaborate gesticulations, fidgety, laid back, when lighting a cigarette, is it from a gold case and lit by a gold lighter, or from a packet and lit with a match); and environment (decor traditional, art nouveau, modern; room elegant, untidy).

5 Taking notes stops your attention wandering while they're speaking.

SHORTHAND

You can't get a staff job as a reporter unless you have shorthand. If you want a job on a newspaper you will probably have to take a Royal Society of Arts exam called a N.V.Q. (National Vocational Qualification: see Chapter 11). You get on-the-job assessment.

One of the seven N.V.Q. performance criteria for interviewing is that – and I quote – 'An accurate and relevant note is taken, including *verbatim* note of appropriate quotes.'

Impromptu interviews

Even if you stay a freelance, there's another reason for shorthand. Should you have to do an impromptu interview you won't have your tape recorder with you, so shorthand is your only means of taking down the answers accurately.

Methods

Both *Pitmans* and *Teeline* systems are taught at many Adult Education Centres. Tuition is also available at colleges throughout the UK.

Here I'm detailing just one college (Pitman's HQ), as an example. Pitman's College, Southampton Row, WC1. Tel: 071 278 6877 teaches:

Pitman's New Era (made up of signs) – the professional journalist's method because it's the fastest (200 words per minute) and the MOST ACCURATE. It takes eighteen weeks to learn attending two evenings weekly.

Pitman's 2,000 (signs) – slightly easier than *New Era* but doesn't reach such high speeds and is not quite as accurate. OK for secretaries who can ask boss to slow down. Eighteen weeks, two evenings weekly. Costs the same as *New Era*

Teeline (alphabet) – easiest of the three but also can't cope with people speaking at great speed. It's also the least accurate to read back. Sixteen weeks, one evening weekly. Costs a little less than the other two methods.

There are teach-yourself books for all of them. Look in your Public Lending Library or bookshops.

Invent your own

If you don't yet know shorthand or have to save up for a dictating machine, don't let that stop you from interviewing – well practising, anyway. While you're learning one of these really effective methods of shorthand it's a good idea to invent your own system.

Mny of t notes fr ths bk ar ritn in my own abbreviated method whch I cn undstnd. Mostly I lv out vowels & use fonetic spelling such as nite, enuf, becos. Y dnt hv to use proper wrds.

True, this only shortens the ordinary words. But it still saves you valuable seconds, leaving more time to spend scribbling the longer words full out.

For a few often used words I write only their initial, e.g. t = the, w = with, tb = to be. A few other words I abbreviate like this: thru = through, lite = light, fite = fight, site = sight, ruf = rough, tuf = tough, ppl = people, btwn = between.

Work out more for yourself. But do be sure you TRANSCRIBE YOUR NOTES IMMEDIATELY. Leave them even till the next day and they'll become illegible.

TAPE RECORDERS

Thank technology for dictating machines or tape recorders, whatever you want to call them. In days of yore there was only shorthand.

Yes, some interviewees might be nervous of them. The best way to handle this is to say: 'You won't mind my recording this, I'm sure – my shorthand's a bit shaky and I don't want to misquote you. You'll agree, it's very important I write what you say and not what I thought you said.' Reassure them that they'll forget the machine is there after a few minutes, after all it's unobtrusive and silent.

Survey

A survey has been carried out on note taking.

Ten interviews were monitored while experienced reporters asked questions and wrote notes (none knew shorthand). At the same time the responses were taped.

Afterwards, on checking the notes against the recording, none of those ten experienced reporters were 100 per cent accurate.

So, despite the fact that a recorder makes some subjects nervous, it's imperative you persuade them to let you use one. You don't want to be sued for misrepresentation after the piece is printed.

Advantages

1   By using a tape recorder, while your subject is speaking you don't have to concentrate on writing his response

verbatim. You can pay full attention to his words, so
you can mentally work out a really incisive follow-up
question.

2   Have you ever tried writing notes while being jostled in a
crowd? You're at a boxing match, on a race course, at the
Olympics – the winner is usually all but trampled under foot
by well wishers and the rest of the journalistic mob. In the
scrum you can hold a mike above their heads and get the
champion's whoops of success.

3   Have you ever tried writing notes whilst clutching a knife
and fork? For this reason try never to do an interview over
a meal. But sometimes it can't be avoided. A restaurant is
one of the least interviewer-friendly venues because of all
the chatter, scrape of cutlery, chink of glasses, moving of
chairs, music, etc that inevitably drown out the interviewee's voice.

4   If your editor is at all incredulous when he receives your
copy, you can prove your subject actually used those words
by playing him the tape.

5   A tape recorder buys you time. Written notes, especially
scribbled longhand, need to be transcribed on to a
typewriter/WP within hours before they become hazy in
your mind and therefore illegible. The longer you leave
them the less the mind can recall. With a recorder you can
transcribe days/weeks later; it's still all there.

Disadvantages

1   If you drop a notebook – it won't break. Try dropping a
tape recorder and see what happens. (Really efficient journalists always take a spare machine.)

2   Background noise. It may not seem too loud at the time,
but often the typewriter in the next room or the hum of the
fluorescent lights can drown or distort speech on the tape.
And you don't find out till you've reached home or your
office. Other intrusive extraneous noises that can play havoc
with a tape are traffic, road works, air conditioning and
piped music. Check before you start the interview. If you
have any doubts, find another room.

If you can't move the interview, ensure you take written notes of really pertinent comments your subject makes.

What to buy

Don't buy a ghetto-blaster the size of a suitcase. And unless you're prepared to pay out £200 to £300, don't buy a weeny miniature.

Over-large – Yes, you reason that it'll have fabulous sound. But you don't need it booming out when you're transcribing. It would also be a right turn-off for your subject to have such an intrusive instrument dumped on their coffee table.

Over-small – Yes, you reason it will be unobtrusive and less likely to frighten your subject. Right. But the cheaper ones are merely toys and suffer greatly from poor sound quality. Also their mini tapes are not very long and break easily. Another minus point about minis – their microphones don't have much range. If you're sitting in any but the first row of a lecture hall you probably can't record the speech. And if you're inter- viewing someone across a wide desk, you may have to thrust the machine under your subject's nose every time he speaks.

Get a pocket-size one – roughly 5in. × 3½in. × 1½in./13cm. × 9cm. × 4cm., prices start around £30. But DO get a reliable make – such a lot depends on it. THOROUGHLY TEST IT IN THE SHOP BEFORE YOU BUY.

Make sure the operating buttons are extremely simple to use – you need to be able to change tapes whilst concentrating on what your subject is saying.

An alarm that sounds when the end of the tape is reached is a useful facility. A flashing light isn't so good as you could miss it because you're watching the interviewee.

And remember to place the recorder where you can see it out of the corner of your eye at least. You need to be able to see that the spools are turning (and if they stop!) – also there should be a light that warns you that the batteries are running low or have run out. There again, as I've just mentioned, you'll be concentrating so much on your subject's words and body language, and on your notebook, you may miss warning lights.

The fail-safe method is to ALWAYS FIT BRAND NEW BATTER-IES before every interview.

Opinions on the joys of having a 'voice activated' model are divided. I had tapes where the voice mysteriously slurred every few minutes. It wasn't until a colleague told me, that I discovered it was caused by the 'voice activator' turning on and off. Many of the slurs distorted the voice so badly that the words were indecipherable.

Batteries/Mains

It's vital that the machine will run on both mains electricity AND battery power.

Mains electricity is much cheaper to use when transcribing. Save your batteries for interviewing. You need an adaptor for mains electricity – it costs about £5.

Buy a recorder that uses EASY-TO-OBTAIN alkaline batteries. Many well-off celebs and specialists live in remote areas of the countryside. If you're interviewing out in the sticks and your machine uses an obscure make or size of battery, you may not be able to buy them.

Always insert NEW batteries for every interview AND take a spare set. Does that sound too much like belt and braces? Well not all batteries have a 'use-by' date on them – they may die on you.

Another reason for buying a machine that is also battery-powered is that you can't rely on plugging into your interviewee's power point:

1 It may take round-pin plugs and yours are square.
2 There may not be one anywhere near where you sit.
3 Even if there is, it fused that morning.
4 They may be too mean to let you use their electricity.

Tapes

Get a recorder that uses easy-to-obtain compact (standard) cassette tapes, not an obscure make or micro-tapes. Get those lasting 60 minutes. The longer 90-minute tapes are more likely to snarl up or break, and 30-minute tapes are so short you have to change them frequently.

And what do you take to every interview? Yes, at least three spare tapes to cope with snarl-ups, breaks and running over time.

Murphy's law also governs tape recorders – all the more reason not to buy a cheap one. (And not being able to do shorthand is another important reason to buy a reliable machine.)

A colleague of mine ALWAYS takes a spare recorder. He specialises in celebrities, many of them American, and they're only over here on brief visits. There's no doing the interview a second time because the machine died on you.

KEEP TAPES AND NOTES

Don't destroy either tapes or written notes. Both should be stored for at least five years with a photocopy of the final piece as printed in the publication. (NB: they don't always print what you write!) At any time the subject could accuse you of mis-quoting. Your only defence when you stand up in court is to produce your notes and tapes.

To give you an example of the importance of this – as I sit writing this, there's a case before the Press Complaints Commission. A sports personality complained that a national newspaper interviewed him and in the printed piece he was

(a) misquoted; and
(b) included were comments he says he never made.

The interviewer, a freelance journalist, was called to produce his notes and tapes. It was revealed that he had altered quotes as well as inventing some, to spice up his story.

This incident doesn't only reflect upon the journalist, but upon the newspaper – whose reputation is also damaged. The editor will have to publish a correction and apology – which undermines the paper's integrity.

This is an example of where keeping tapes and notes worked to the detriment of the journalist; but if he'd been ethical, it would have been to his benefit.

Two final points about storing material:

1   Yes, your profile/feature has been published and is now history. But you never know if you will have to write about the person or topic again – even if only briefly. Tapes and notes of an interview can be excellent reference sources.

2   You also might one day want to write a book about the person you interviewed. The tapes and notes would be invaluable.

CAMERA

A picture is worth a thousand words. This isn't obligatory, of course, but a recent mug shot (portrait) of your celebrity or specialist can add interest and value to your written piece.

Learn how to use your camera. Make yourself familiar with it so you don't look amateur in front of your interviewee. It's worth getting a book on basic photography from the library.

A professional photographer always takes at least three close-ups – the subject looking to the right, to the left, and straight into the camera. Practise with half a dozen films. Take close-up shots of friends in various poses. This will also make you practise putting people at ease because 90 per cent of the population hate having their photo taken.

FINAL CONTINGENCIES

Just before you leave, check that you have your interviewee's address and phone number plus a phone card and small change.

Cars, tubes, buses, trains can all break down or have other delays. On the way to the interview you may have to phone to apologise that you're going to be late.

And the ultimate reassurance – go to the loo. You can't effectively take notes while you're sitting there squirming.

EXERCISE

Select a radio programme where there's a talk. Take down five minutes word for word (time yourself).

Do the same with nine other, DIFFERENT programmes and see if you get down more words the tenth time than the first.

CHAPTER 13

Meeting your Interviewee

- Arrive on time
- You must be in control
- How you feel
- Role play
- Confidence boosters
- What to wear
- How they feel

- Body language
- Even the famous
- Vital first minutes
- Starting the actual interview – 14 tips
- Exercise.

PROFESSIONAL INTERVIEWERS are courteous and arrive punctually. You KNOW how bad traffic conditions are – don't trust to luck, set out half an hour before you need to.

Another reason for punctuality – your time is precious, and so is that of your interviewee. It could well be that s/he has another appointment directly after the one with you. So if they've said, 'I can give you an hour, come at 3PM', it could be because of a tight work schedule. They are seeing someone else at 4PM.

If you arrive too early, go and have a cuppa or take a stroll around taking notes about the neighbourhood. For profiles particularly, it's valuable to know a little about the environment in which your subject lives. A description of the smart/sleazy/rural surroundings will add colour to the write-up.

YOU MUST BE IN CONTROL

To get maximum co-operation, professional journalists plan to create an atmosphere of maximum calm and harmony so the interviewee will feel good and give a friendly response. Otherwise the interviewer won't be in CONTROL, which is vital. This is a big persuasion job.

You apply psychology from the start – from the minute you put your finger on the doorbell. Greet your interviewee with a friendly smile, firm handshake and possibly a low-key compliment such as: 'Lovely garden – do you do it yourself?'

If they've come to you, say: 'Hope you had an easy journey – let's start with a cup of coffee.' WELCOME them.

HOW YOU FEEL

Well OK – that's all very fine. But knowing what to do and actually DOING IT can be two different things. What gets in the way is fear (I mentioned this in Chapter 9).

Let's first get one thing clear. YOU'RE VERY LIKELY EQUALLY TERRIFIED OF EACH OTHER.

What I'm telling you now is:

(a) How to cope with your own nervousness;
(b) How to help your interviewee cope with theirs.

I know most beginner journalists are scared silly when they arrive for their first interview. How do I know? Because this isn't merely an academic book. It deals realistically with real people. At the beginning of each journalism course I ask my students what they want to know about interviewing. Time and time again they ask: 'How do you overcome your nervousness?'

Adrenalin Any meeting with a stranger sets your adrenalin going. This is from the days when we lived in caves. You reach the doorstep and you start to feel apprehensive. But tell yourself: 'Don't be a twit, I'm only going to talk to another human being.'

OK, so you've convinced yourself you haven't got to face an enemy – that makes your adrenalin stop flowing. But the chemical released by your original apprehension is still loose in the body, you will still feel hyped up – nervous. So BEFORE you ring the doorbell, you disperse the adrenalin by taking several

deep breaths. To help you remember, glue into your memory
BESS – Breathe, Eyes, Shoulders, Smile.

B   Breathe – take three deep breaths;
E   Eyes – close them;
S   Shoulders – straighten them and drop them;
S   Smile – Open your eyes and SMILE. Tell yourself: 'I know
what I'm doing, there's no need to be scared.'

You go in there smiling and looking confident – therefore
you're automatically in control.

If you have a personal problem that day, you keep it out of
your professional life. So you've split with your other half, your
cat died yesterday, you've got to go to court for a parking
offence, you've got the curse – TOUGH.

You carry on playing the confident journalist all through the
interview – and your interviewee won't challenge you.

You don't need to TELL them you're in charge. They're
prepared subconsciously, before you arrive, to meet a compet-
ent interviewer. In other words, they expect a professional
journalist. AND THAT'S WHAT YOU GIVE THEM. They've no
way of knowing this is your first interview.

From the moment you arrive they already have confidence
in you – AS LONG AS YOU SHOW BY YOUR CONFIDENT,
AMIABLE DEMEANOUR that you're a person whom they can
trust and can rely on to handle the interview professionally.

ROLE PLAY

What you're doing is role-playing.

Don't let this role-play concept throw you. We all do it
subconsciously all the time – it's the way we react to the
person we're with. The people who attend my classes role-
play, so do I. They role-play students and I the tutor. None
of us plays these roles permanently, only when we're in
class.

They role-play by doing what students do – sit behind desks,
take notes, ask questions. I KNOW WHAT BEHAVIOUR TO

EXPECT FROM THEM. They know what to expect from me –
to teach them journalism. In fact, they expect me, and more
important they ALLOW me, to be in control.

Do you see how it's just the same with interviewing? The
interviewee expects and allows you to be in control. But
if you don't do it from the outset THEY will take over –
just as unruly pupils will take over a class if the teacher is
weak.

So at the interview, establish confident control from the word
go. Your subject expects you to ask questions and expects to
answer them. They take their cue from you – and everything
runs smoothly.

CONFIDENCE BOOSTERS

1 You're clutching that long list of questions.
2 You've thoroughly researched – you're ready for any questions they may throw at you.
3 You know you can rely on your equipment because you
   tested it and checked it before you left.
4 Possibly you went on that assertiveness course.
5 You look good . . .

WHAT TO WEAR

More psychology: your initial visual impact is important, so
give some thought to how you'll DRESS.

Wear something you FEEL good in – that helps give you
confidence.

Also, try to predict their reaction and dress in a compatible
style. If interviewing a pop star you could wear designer
casuals. If it's a business executive or a consultant cardiologist, wear a suit. If you know the person's elderly don't turn
up in a leather miniskirt and screaming green hair (especially
if you're a fella) – clothes are a part of role-playing.

How They Feel

As I've just mentioned, they're just as terrified of you as you are (were!) of them, even if it doesn't show. The thought of being interviewed by a journalist is daunting. They're in the hot seat. Even if they're used to being interviewed, they don't know what to expect from you.

If you don't put them at their ease, anxiety could paralyse their brain and their lips, and you'll come away without the information you need.

A Human Being   Many student interviewers give themselves problems because they see their interviewee merely as a bucket of information, and not as a person.

They forget that here's a human being, just like themselves, who has likes and dislikes; off days and on days; problems on their minds from 'the milkman didn't call today' to 'this week the building society repossess my home'.

Additionally, they have personalities. They could welcome someone asking them questions or hate their guts.

Their problems and personalities affect the way in which they will behave towards you. Don't be scared of what you might encounter or you could be a brainless jelly by the time you arrive. Merely be aware that it's a real live person you're meeting – respect their foibles and shortcomings. You made the request for the meeting – they're doing you a favour.

Body Language

Ninety-nine people out of a hundred will be nervous of you. Those with the highest degree of apprehension will be 'ordinary, non-famous' people. Second highest scorers are specialists. Celebs have usually been interviewed before, several times, so have overcome much of the anxiety.

Facial expressions may not tell you how scared they are as these are more easily controlled. Watch their body language.

If they're sitting obviously tense, how would this manifest itself? What could they be doing to show they feel threatened? They may have their arms clasped over their chest, or be constantly fidgeting with something, or have clenched hands, or be avoiding eye contact. Look for these signs. The visual message to you is: 'I feel threatened.'

So you reassure them. Tell them to relax. Make them feel important. You could say: 'I bet you're not as nervous as me.' Chat casually for a bit till they relax and drop their hands into their lap.

You could leave your notebook and tape recorder in your briefcase initially and chat in a friendly way – 'That's an elegant vase, was it a present?' 'Is that a photo of your daughter?' 'The garden looks pretty from here, did you choose the plants?' 'What an enormous cat, what's his name?' Anything non-threatening.

They may have a small problem that they mention – 'the boy didn't deliver my *Guardian* today' or 'my son's left his bike/skis in the hall again' or 'the Council won't repair the pavement outside my gate'. Sympathise – let them have their whinge, it all helps establish the start of a rapport with you.

And very important – don't mispronounce their name. It can be a real put down. Practise saying it before you arrive.

EVEN THE FAMOUS

Even Big Names can be nervous – it's surprising how many are. You get shy celebs as well as arrogant ones.

Sometimes it's because of bad treatment by a journalist in the past. You need to convey right from the word go that you're not into 'jugular journalism'. You're going to be frank but not vicious.

I remember Anna-Marie, a student of mine. She told me: 'I did my very first interview this week. I went to see X, the film producer who's made three box office raves and got two Academy Awards.

'When I got to his house he said: "Let's have some tea." His wife brought in a teapot and cakes and we all sat round talking of the weather and the latest Royals scandal.

'Then he said: "I'd like to show you our new conservatory." So I admired the pine finish and the cyclamen.

'Then he asked: "Have you seen this book on how to land-scape a garden?" And the penny dropped. He was avoiding like mad – he was terrified.

'I just didn't believe it – all the signs were there. He was scared of ME of all people, a first-time interviewer, though he didn't know that, of course. And he's so famous. But there he was, looking desperate and keeping finding things to do rather than let the interview start.'

Having an interviewee scared of you is a great disadvantage. Their anxiety clouds their brain and they're unable to respond to you amiably and intelligently. You won't get very good quotes. Look for the signs and REASSURE them.

VITAL FIRST MINUTES

In the first few minutes of an interview a tremendous amount happens. On the surface you're greeting each other, then asking/answering questions.

On another level you're both working hard at assessing each other. While you're asking the initial easy questions all your antennae are out waving – picking up their mood (suspicious, anxious, affable, surly, aggressive).

As I'm on your side, I'm telling you how to come out on top.

STARTING THE ACTUAL INTERVIEW

1 Be careful not to be over-familiar with your subject – especially if you're meeting them for the first time. Examples of over-familiarity that you'd avoid:

(a) Don't smoke or chew gum.

(b) It's better not to call them by their first name until they invite you to.

(c) And certainly, don't TOUCH them – especially if they're of the opposite sex. We all have an area of 'personal space' into which we allow only intimates such as our mother or lover. Don't invade this.

(d) If in their place, be the perfect guest. Don't overstep the marks of courtesy and respect. It all boils down to good manners.

2 Fidgeting conveys nervousness. It's also irritating for your interviewee. He won't tell you what you want to know unless he likes you. Sit comfortably so you don't have to keep shifting.

But don't slouch, that could also irritate him. Sit with a straightish back and both feet firmly on the floor – it looks business-like and is quietly dominant.

About halfway through you should have enough of a rapport going, so you can lean back and cross your legs.

Where you sit is important

3 Part of being in control – even though at the interviewee's place – is arranging where you SIT. Eye contact is very important. But don't sit immediately opposite – that comes over as a confrontation. And don't sit side by side as you'll both get a crick in your neck. Sit at about 45 degrees.

Don't sit too close – they'll feel threatened. Or too far away, you'll seem remote. Wait till they sit, THEN arrange YOUR chair. They'll often ask: 'Is it OK to sit here?'

And pay attention to the height of your chair. Remember that straight-backed, armless chairs are always higher than upholstered armchairs. Sitting higher is dominant – having to look up at someone is always a psychological disadvantage.

If they are the timid type, accept the armchair they will probably offer. Then they won't have to look up to you. If they come over a bit cocksure, try and get them to sit in the armchair while you take the straighter, higher one.

Test Your Machine Again

4   Before you start, ALWAYS ask if you can test your tape recorder. There are three good reasons for this.

(a) It's no good discovering afterwards that the tape is blank. If your tape recorder doesn't work, then use the spare machine you've taken.

(b) It also strangely helps them relax because having to test the machine demonstrates that you're a vulnerable human being.

(c) This is when you make sure they're happy about you using the machine – 'My note taking isn't so great, do you mind? I don't want to misquote you.'

5   Another practical tip – always take off your wristwatch and put it on the table in front of you. This saves you having to keep lifting your sleeve, which can be off-putting because they will feel you're either bored or are hurrying them.

6   If you sit relaxed this should help *them* relax. Never sit on the edge of your chair and fire questions at them just because you've seen a reporter do it on TV. That's pure theatre – it's not like that in real life.

7   Don't be shy of showing you have a list of questions – it looks professional. It shows you've put in some thought about them – they'll be flattered.

Don't Talk Too Much

8   Aim at a two-way chat atmosphere, except that you don't do much of the chatting. Only 10 to 15 per cent of the tape should be your voice. Use your questions in the way that a theatre prompt uses a script – control the situation so THEY do the talking, so THEY give you the info that's essential to making your written feature or profile SALEABLE.

9   They'll respond better to you if you make it obvious you're following their comments. How would you do this?

Good eye contact, occasionally nod, occasionally repeat what they've said. They'll be more co-operative if they feel you're interested in what they have to say. Your position of strength is that most people like to give their opinions. And HOWEVER BORING they might be, they might lead to an interesting comment.

Warm Them Up

10 They'll need warming up – need convincing you're a nice guy and aren't going to grill them. How would you do this? What types of QUESTIONS would you ask to start off with?

Begin with a few pretty ordinary ones, those that are very easy to answer, so they get through the first few minutes thinking: 'Well, this isn't so awful after all.'

If an 'ordinary' non-famous person, ask them where they were born and what the village/town was like then. Can they remember their first school, and what was that like?

If talking to a specialist you could start with questions about their company, hospital or institute. Try 'When was it founded, and by whom?'

If you're face-to-face with a Big Name, then start with something about their profession: 'I saw your last film/play (or read your last book, or saw you play against Arsenal) – was it the most challenging one you've ever faced?' You can also subtly show you've done your homework by saying: 'You went to school in Paris, didn't you? Was it a large/progressive/old-fashioned school?' (And see Point 11.)

It doesn't matter whether or not you're going to USE the answers to these initial questions in your write-up. The objective at this stage of the interview is not 'getting information' but 'establishing rapport'.

Follow those questions with other easily-answered ones to which you already know the answers through research – then they'll merely be confirming. This gives you the opportunity to mentally assess them, to guess how the interview will develop, and be ready to field any googlies they might lob at you.

Although your first questions need to be uncomplicated, don't let them be superficial. Your subject will quickly become bored and won't give you their whole attention or best reactions. Keep the difficult questions till later, when they've learned to trust you. Work up to these more pertinent questions with QUIET CONFIDENCE.

Asking simple questions at the outset also helps them stop being aware of 'that infernal machine' that's squatting on the coffee table recording every word. After a short while they'll become so involved with answering your increasingly probing questions that they'll forget the presence of the little black box.

When the tape recorder is in position, switch it on and don't touch it again till you need to turn over the tape. If you keep fiddling with the sound level and other buttons this will draw their attention to it.

11 As an opening gambit you might try something casual like: 'I only just made it. They cancelled the train I planned to catch. Have you ever had a train cancelled?' Quite probably they have. They'll tell you about it – and you've established mutual empathy. This is a very good platform from which to step into the rest of the interview.

But you need to have your sixth sense alert as to whether this is the best approach for THIS person. Some people will just stonewall you if you attempt to get chummy. Busy and egotistical people will prefer to get straight down to business without any preamble.

Give Them Time to Answer

12 If they're ultra-nervous and you haven't been able to thaw them out sufficiently to unlock their lips – try giving them time. When they're silent after a question don't hassle them – don't immediately jump in with another question. Don't be afraid to sit and wait so they have TIME TO THINK before they answer.

13 If at the beginning your subject wants to tell you their troubles – let them. As long as you don't allow it to go on too long. At least they're revealing, and this makes it easier for you later.

But keep an eye on your watch. If you've agreed an interview of an hour you can only let them ramble on a little before you need to say enthusiastically: 'Really, that's interesting, I'd like to return to that later. But may we now start on these few questions I've brought?'

Don't Forget That Write-Up

14 And among all this mental, physical and verbal activity at the start of the interview, never forget that it's only a means to an end – THE FINAL WRITTEN PIECE. If you leave the interview without enough details to write a saleable feature or profile, then you've failed.

To be a successful interviewer, you must focus on several levels concurrently:

(a) Continually analyse the mood of the interviewee so you can 'turn up' or 'turn down' your delivery/tone of voice.
(b) Scan the list of questions.
(c) Listen to the answers so you can follow with a relevant question. Often you can repeat the interviewee's last couple of words, then say: 'And then?' or 'Why?'
(d) Remember the structure of the piece you're going to write so you can steer the questions towards getting answers that will make it SALEABLE.

EXERCISE

Write down welcoming/complimentary greetings you would use for:

1 Celebrity – A tennis champion;
2 Specialist – A consultant radiologist;
3 Ordinary/non-famous person – someone who has won £1 million on the pools.

These should all be quite different from each other.

CHAPTER 14

Interview Techniques

- Rapport
- Listen to the answers
- First impressions
- Don't kill the golden goose
- The non-anecdote
- Aggression
- Hard-nosed
- Leading questions
- Coarse fishing
- Age and weight
- The Waiting Game
- Sympathy
- Be non-committal
- Off the record
- Personal questions
- How deep should you probe?
- Facts – your criteria
- Exercise.

Is INTERVIEWING an art or a craft?

In all journalists' hands it is a craft. It becomes an art when the writer uses their individual creativity.

All art starts off as a craft, i.e. something anyone can learn. For example, the opera singer has to first learn music theory and vocal technique; the ballerina needed to learn steps; the master artist had to practise mixing colours and applying them to the paper; the best-selling writer needed basic grammar, punctuation and spelling.

The same goes for the interviewer. The skills/craft is in this book. What turns any craft into an art, makes it successful, is the ability to execute the mechanics to a superlative level of excellence and superiority in your own individual style.

It's pretty obvious that the more you interview the better you become. So don't sink into despair should your first few interviews not come up to your expectations. Try and get in the practice with friends I outlined in Chapter 9.

RAPPORT

A successful interview is NOT:

(a) an interrogation;
(b) a friendly chat.

It falls uniquely between the two. The French have a word for it – rapport.

Chambers dictionary's definition of rapport is: 'relation, connection, sympathy, emotional bond'. The Oxford dictionary says: 'communication, relationship, connection'. And Cassell's dictionary: 'correspondence, sympathetic relationship, agreement, harmony'.

Mesh all these and you leave the interview with a tape full of quotable quotes – and the profile/feature practically writes itself.

A successful interviewer is a subtle investigator.

And interviewing is manipulative. You may not like to admit that. But as long as you use the information you get ETHICALLY, there's no demerit. It's a little bit like money. There's nothing wrong with wealth – it's how it's used that sometimes makes it immoral.

LISTEN TO THE ANSWERS

A very serious mistake that practically all beginners make is that they don't LISTEN TO THE REPLIES. This is because they're grimly focusing on the next question on their list. They rely on their machines to record the response which they can listen to later.

But later, when the interviewee's gone, YOU CAN'T FOLLOW-UP. There's little point in saying to the empty air: 'That's an interesting point, could you elaborate on that?'

So concentrate on what your subject is saying so you can:

(a) formulate the next question;
(b) mentally fashion the final write-up.

Example   The non-creative interviewer is inflexible:

Question   How long have you been a full-time novelist?
Answer   For four years – since I left my nine-to-five job.
Q   How many books have you written? ignoring the nucleus of the answer. If he'd left that question for later and followed up with: 'Tell me about your job,' he'd have got:

'I was a physiotherapist in a large hospital. About a month before I was made redundant – I didn't leave of my own accord – I was given seven patients to treat who were all in the same hospice. Most of them were bedridden, all had severely restricted movement. I discovered just how much they relied on books, magazines and newspapers.

'None of them were all that keen on TV, they said, as they had to look at the programme when it was on and not when they were ready to watch it. With a book, it could be taken up at any time – even in the middle of the night. And they all loved 'a good read'.

'I'd always dabbled at writing – getting nowhere. It was the coincidence of being made redundant and seeing how important books were to these people that motivated me to write my first novel.

'And the hospice was full of people with wonderful life stories to tell. That's where I got a lot of the character studies for my novels.'

And that adds a pertinent and interesting anecdote to your final write-up.

So when you're face to face with your subject, don't rush. THINK about the answer you've just had and let it prompt your next question.

That interviewers don't listen to the answers, so they can react to what has just been said with a follow-up question, is a lament of Jean Silvan-Evans, Senior Lecturer in Journalism at the University of Wales. She stresses:

'The answers are supposed to go through your mind before they go through your pen. Otherwise, what's the point of sending an expensive journalist to the interview? The editor could well have sent the office junior with a tape recorder.'

So when the interviewee has finished speaking, don't automatically and blindly come out with the next question on your list. Mentally assess the value of the response you've just had. Can it be improved by you asking: 'Could you enlarge on that?'

Take:

(a) the science of journalism; and
(b) controlled, contemplative interviewing; and
(c) unique, creative flair,

and you have an ART.

The professional interviewer doesn't walk in and reel off the list of questions as though it were a shopping list. No, they walk in acutely aware of their interviewee and the surroundings. Although they act like a person merely asking questions, they are concurrently analysing their subject's psyche and personality. This way they know what demeanour to adopt, what tone of voice, when to smile, when to be insistent, when to be restrained. It's an essential part of being in control.

FIRST IMPRESSIONS

Be aware that it's not only you who's doing all that stuff I mentioned in the previous chapter to gain and retain control. You're both trying to impress each other. Your interviewee won't be (or will seldom be) trying to control the interview, but they WILL be concentrating on looking good in your write-up.

Some first impressions should be listened to with a sceptical ear as things aren't always what they seem to be (e.g. 'The sun comes up and the sun goes down' – it doesn't, does it?)

Example Author Fanella Fiction has written a novel that's a success in the UK. But apart from one novel the interviewer hasn't been able to find anything else with Fanella's by-line on it.

In answer to the question: 'What else have you had published?' Fanella says: 'Oh quite a lot of stuff – I've many years' experience.'

That sounds quite impressive. Until the journalist asks: 'Can you be more specific, please?'

The reply will probably be (relying on you not to check): 'A few features in the nationals – *Guardian*, *Independent* – you know the sort of thing,' which, said with panache, persuades the interviewer to go on to the next question. Fanella's response would seldom, if ever, be the truth: 'Well, I've had articles in my tennis club newsletter, as well as a poem in my parish magazine.'

But the professional, incisive journalist follows with: 'Have you any cuttings I could see, please? I'd like to mention them in the profile.'

DON'T KILL THE GOLDEN GOOSE

There's a huge difference between being incisive, but fair, and being vicious. After a successful interview it's better that your subject is left feeling you're a nice guy, than as if they've had a trip in the washer-drier. You never know when you will need to interview this specialist, victim or celebrity again.

Example For a piece in your local paper, you interview a woman who's been burgled. A year later that same woman is burgled again. This time she was in the house and was threatened with rape.

Will she welcome you back and give you all the highly readable details, or will she refuse to see you because you were so unsympathetic last time?

Example The specialist you interview today about the start of the design of a refinery, you may well need to contact when his magnum project has been completed.

Example   The star you interview today about her latest film, may well be someone you have to see again when her next film is released.

THE NON-ANECDOTE

Anecdotes are meat and drink to writers of profiles and features. You get a real buzz when you feel one is coming up.

Example   Your subject says: 'I owe a great deal of my success to my friends.' Great, you think. But a swift analysis shows that s/he hasn't really said anything at all.

You must follow up with: 'Exactly what do you mean by that?'

'Oh, my friends' magnanimity – you know.'

An improvement, but still too obscure.

'Can you give me a few instances of this magnanimity – what they actually did?'

'Oh well, Heather – she lent me her cottage in Scotland when I needed absolute peace and quiet to write the "Travels in the World's most famous Mountain Ranges" series. And Martin – he and his wife Gill actually took my two children off my hands for the entire summer holidays. Or I'd never have got the series done.

'I mean, I didn't lose contact. The cottage isn't on the phone so Martin got them to write to me every other day, and I wrote back to them. Those are letters I'll always treasure. I kept every one of them.'

So with a bit of persistent probing you got a little gem of an anecdote.

AGGRESSION

Never be conceited enough to antagonise your subject.

Example   'So what's so special about you, Mr Megastar? You seem a pretty ordinary person to me' – compared with: 'Your

fans rave about you – can you put your finger on the special
quality you have? Is it sheer charisma, talent or what?'

Even if you feel he's an insufferable bore, you don't ask the
first one. Unless you want to be told: 'Get stuffed.' The second
question could well get the reaction of a modest lowering of
the eyes followed by a revealing account of all the hard work,
rejection, disappointments they had on the way up.

I'm certainly not suggesting a 'Uriah Heep' act from you
merely because he's a Big Name. Just be courteously
objective.

HARD-NOSED

I've already mentioned that I ask students starting my courses
to list what they want to know about interviewing. (Many of
the questions are listed at the beginning of this book.) But one
I didn't include in the Top Forty was: 'How do you apply
hard-nosed, aggressive interview techniques?'

I assume this student wanted to be a political journalist or a
crime reporter.

In the first place, you'd need to be naturally aggressive.
Otherwise, don't bother – I doubt if you can learn how to adopt
a personality trait from a book. Then, as with any particular
field of journalism, study the nationals and pick out news stories and news features you'd like to have written.

Then you merely work backwards. There on the page is the
information. You need to work out the questions that would
have been asked to get those answers.

LEADING QUESTIONS

One method of steering the interview in the direction you want
it to go is to use leading questions. These verbally trap the
subject into giving the reply the journalist wants. And some
are not entirely ethical because they're subtle bullying. Well,
it depends on the subject, of course.

Example   Version 1 is an open question, version 2 is a leading question:

1   'What did you think of Sid Striker's latest performance against Arsenal?'
2   'Sid Striker's latest match against Arsenal was pathetic, wasn't it?'

Example   Another type of leading question puts the subject in a position where they can't really disagree.

'The Government recently released a report giving some horrific statistics on the number of deaths on the roads caused by drivers who were under the influence of alcohol. Would you say drinking and driving should be outlawed?' The interviewee hasn't really a choice of answer, has he? He'll obviously say 'Yes'. Which leaves him wide open for: 'You're drinking alcohol now and your car parked outside isn't chauffeur-driven. How will you get home?'

If the interviewee hasn't enough sense to say: 'I'm going to call a taxi', then the write-up will probably read like this: 'Despite Joe Bloggs's statement, "Yes, drinking and driving should be outlawed", after downing four double whiskies he drove his car home.'

And Joe Bloggs will sue you for libel.

But you see what I mean about leading questions being subtle bullying?

The above example was a double-think on behalf of the journalist. On one mental level he was concentrating on asking questions. On level two he was structuring the piece he had to write in his head. Joe Bloggs wasn't giving him the answers he wanted, so he suggested some.

And the libel. Yes, all that was written was indeed true. So how can Bloggs sue? But that's not what libel is all about. It's not what is written that is suable, it's the EFFECT it has on the plaintiff.

COARSE FISHING

An experienced interviewer plays his subject like an angler plays a game fish.

When the answer goes on and on and gets completely off
the subject, always haul him back with a selection from these
verbal lines:

'Fascinating. I wonder if we could now get on to XXX.'

'That's great. Could we now look at my next question?'

'Right, but I'd like to return to the point we were discussing
earlier.'

AGE AND WEIGHT

I've never been too keen on asking ages – or a person's weight.
They will usually lie, especially women, so the answer won't
be any use to you. Only ask them if they are very, very
young/thin or very, very old/fat – that's the only reason it could
be of interest.

THE WAITING GAME

If you ask a question and they don't answer straight away,
WAIT. Don't immediately jump in with another question.
There's nothing wrong with a little silence.

You'll both sit there, the embarrassment mounting on both
sides as the silence stretches. But you were the last to speak,
so the silence is their problem, not yours. So hang on in there.
Let embarrassment nudge them into answering.

But If They're Nervous

However, they could be tongue-tied because of nervousness.
Help them. Here's another use for the classic: 'Would you say
that . . .' approach, which requires only a 'yes' or 'no' reply.
If you try a few of these your subject will gradually gain enough
confidence to add relevant comments.

Example 'Did you have much trouble raising that £1,500 for
Cancer Research?'

She's over-modest and doesn't know how to answer. So she frowns and stays silent. You try again.

'Some people find fund-raising easy, for others it's an uphill slog; how was it for you?'

'I don't know.' She's desperately shy, beginning to feel foolish and looks distressed.

'Would you say fund-raising was difficult?'

'Yes.'

'OK. You're doing fine. Now, would you say it needs a lot of hard work and long hours?'

'Yes.'

'And what did you do to raise the money?'

'Car boot sales.'

By saying 'yes' she has agreed to the words you used – BUT ONLY THOSE SHE HEARD YOU SPEAK, REMEMBER. Play fair. So in your news story you can legitimately write: 'The £1,500 raised for Cancer Research by Jane Smith wasn't an easy undertaking. She admitted: "It was hard work and meant long hours organising the car boot sales." '

SYMPATHY

Sympathy/compliance often results in good quotes.

Your subject may have some sort of grievance or relate a harrowing experience. Follow up with one of these:

'Did you really? That must have taken some courage.'

'Yes, a lot of people are with you on that.'

'You obviously feel strongly about this.'

When you've shown by your tone of voice you're on their side, they often respond with a bit of soul-baring. And notice, you didn't AGREE with them. You didn't have to, you merely showed you were understanding.

Additionally, sympathising with your subject in this way can motivate them to open up with a great deal of 'delicate' information. They become a little careless. They think: 'Oh, she's one of us, she won't quote me on this.'

But you do.

It's a favourite journalistic ploy. You were careful, of course, not to say anywhere: 'I won't use this.' So it's an assumption on their part and grist for your mill.

BE NON-COMMITTAL

If you strongly disagree with a point they're making, it's not up to you to show it. Be impartial. You're not crusading, you're interviewing – whether you agree or disagree with their viewpoint is irrelevant. You're a reporter; your job is to report the facts.

Whether you agree or disagree, be non-committal. Merely nod and say: 'I see.' You don't need to say any more. The nod shows you registered what they said and wish them to continue.

OFF THE RECORD

Of course, if your subject precedes a statement with: 'This is off the record', you immediately show by very positive action that it is. You switch off your machine and put down your notebook and ballpoint. This is a gentleman's agreement, and one you'll honour as a professional journalist.

It doesn't mean that the rest of the interview is off the record. When your interviewee has finished the statement s/he doesn't want you to record, s/he'll let you turn on your machine again. If s/he forgets, merely ask: 'Is it OK to turn the machine back on now?'

It could be, of course, that the 'off the record' statement is libellous – so you wouldn't have used it anyway.

Sometimes 'off the record' has a 'deadline'. I once interviewed a film star who told me she was planning a simply fabulous surprise birthday party for another top star. She followed that with: 'Of course, that's off the record.' As my piece was being published in a newspaper two days later I had to agree. But should my profile have been for a glossy monthly magazine not published until after the party date, then I could have used the information.

Nobody can live in isolation if they work in publishing. Word gets around about how ethical you are.

If you can build up a reputation for discretion when necessary and when asked for it, you'll gain nothing but respect. And a celebrity who has vetoed all interviews because of previous unscrupulous treatment by a journalist, may make an exception with you. And that's how you get an exclusive.

See also pages 166–7.

PERSONAL QUESTIONS

An unobtrusive way of obtaining a revealing personal answer is to ask a general question first.

Example   Your research told you that your interviewee had a teenage son.

'How much pocket money do you think a fourteen-year-old should be given?'

'About £5 a week.'

'That's feasible. How much do you give your son?'

'Oh well – officially he gets £5 – but unofficially it's always more. There's so many things he needs, or thinks he needs.'

'But if you've stipulated £5 shouldn't you stick to it?'

'I fear that if I don't give it to him he might find other methods of getting the CD or trainers or whatever. There's such a sinister peer pressure, it could drive some kids to petty crime even.'

And there you have a very usable quote.

NB: See also Chapter 15, ALARM BELLS.

HOW DEEP SHOULD YOU PROBE?

There's no one answer to this question. The depth of your inquisition is always determined by the justification of your quest.

It depends so much on what kind of write-up you're aiming for after the interview, what field you're in. If it's one of the serious ones – foreign affairs, politics, finance, war correspondent – any of those justify pretty profound probing.

On the other hand you might have decided you want to be a gossip columnist where you write about the rich, famous and silly. Here you have to learn how to be a sneak.

A journalist has no right to be judge and jury. But many beginners dream of the spectacular exposé they're going to do one day.

As I can't be at your elbow when you're doing the actual interview, I can only leave 'to probe or not to probe' to your own integrity.

Here's a way of tackling just one point. This needs accurate instinct from you, but many subjects will reveal valuable truths merely to put you right. Particularly with the tetchy topic of money. This is a 'leading question', of course.

Example   'It's rumoured you got a £75,000 advance on that book, is that true?'
'Oh no.'
'OK, I'll put the record straight for you – how much was it?'
'£80,000.'
The £75,000 was merely a calculated guess. But it got the desired result because it appealed to their pride. And the follow-up question showed the journalist wanted to help them maintain their reputation. And the interviewee fell for it.

People will also often tell you the correct amount because they're afraid you'll mention an incorrect one if they don't.

FACTS – YOUR CRITERIA

What keeps the ethical journalist on the straight and narrow are facts. That's what the reading public expect, not fabrication.

'Ah, BUT' I can hear you say. 'It's the way the facts are handled that MAKE the story.' Right. And your future reputation as a journalist rests on this. Only you can decide whether you want to be an ethical journalist or adopt the gutter press tactics of not letting the facts get in the way of a good story.

The decision isn't a simple one. Every journalist who interviews a scientist has the word 'breakthrough' glued into their brain. If it's a sportsman, the word is 'record breaker', if a rock singer, it's 'chart-topper'. We're all easily seduced by Press clichés. So are the public. That's what they want to read – near-misses don't make news.

The temptation to over-embellish the facts is often too much for the beginner journalist to resist. Hence they write: 'The 20,000 sales of Samantha Saga's first novel made it a runaway best-seller.' This indicates that thousands of copies of the book were snatched up by the eager public the minute it came into the shops. The truth is that yes, 20,000 copies of the novel were sold – but that was over a ten-year period.

You don't develop a reputation of integrity by wilfully distorting the facts.

EXERCISE

1 Write down three leading questions (on any topic).
2 Re-phrase them so they're unbiased.

CHAPTER 15

Problems at the Interview

- Delicate questions
- Alarm bells
- The Veto
- Off the record
- Personal gaffe
- Censorship
- Bombshell
- The Big Name
- The Little Name
- Neurotics

- Politicians
- Gone cold
- Uninterest
- Taciturnity
- Verbal deluge
- Digresser
- Lob it back
- Swallowers
- Exercise.

YOU'RE READING this book for a formula, for a nice set of rules to follow. Yes, I give you many guidelines and tips based on my own and colleagues' experiences. But none of us have done the interview(s) YOU are going to do.

Each interview is unique. That's much of the fascination, the excitement. Each presents a different challenge.

Many will have the problems presented in this book. But some will have problems I've never encountered or even dreamed of because each interviewee is individual in some way.

Be prepared to meet a singular situation each time. Your best safety net is not to let yourself become complacent about all the preparation. Otherwise, at any of your interviews you could meet a situation that will give you a great deal of unnecessary distress.

The rest of this chapter shows you how to deal with some fairly predictable problems.

DELICATE QUESTIONS

Questions concerning drugs, sex, AIDS, bribery, adultery, big money, death, alcoholism and other emotive topics must be handled tactfully and gently. Even though it's foremost in your mind, you can't start with: 'Hello, nice of you to agree to an interview. Are you gay?'

Delicate questions aren't asked until you're well into the interview and have got a decent rapport going as well as a goodly slice of their trust.

And you don't trample on your subject's vulnerability with hobnail boots.

This is another area where you call loudly on your sensitivity. By three-quarters of the way through the interview you should have got to know the person pretty well. You've been watching the signals – body language, tone of voice, facial expressions, eye contact.

Only your intuition can tell you when (or whether) they are ready to be asked The Big Question, the one you REALLY came for. That's the one that's going to lead off your write-up and make it irresistible to that editor.

Another reason to leave touchy questions till well into the meeting is that the reaction could be that your subject throws you out. So make sure you have enough answers for your profile/news feature before you ask the Biggy.

Some people react most favourably to a direct approach. With others they could be shocked into silence or automatic denial or fury, so they need a more roundabout approach. Creative questioning is deciding which strategy, then wording your Big Question with care.

You may have to sugar the pill with ambiguity. But then the answer might also be ambiguous. So you're no further forward unless you follow-up with: 'By that you mean XXX?' You can't sell ambiguity to an editor.

ALARM BELLS

Try putting yourself in your interviewee's shoes. This mental role-playing is part of preparation when you're planning your questions. Imagine someone asking you: 'Are you sleeping with your sister?' Note your own reactions this minute. All your alarm bells are clanging, aren't they?

So work out a gentle, altruistic approach that doesn't assault the emotions.

Example For instance, don't be JUDGMENTAL in the way in which you ask. You're doing a profile on an Olympic contestant.

Don't say: 'I understand you have a problem. Is it true you smoke grass?' They may not see it as a problem. And if they have any sense they also won't admit it, as it's illegal in this country. Try:

'Relaxation must be difficult for a high-achiever like you who must have to train about 15 hours a day. Some people consider the occasional joint is a great relaxant – would you agree?'

If they say: 'Yes,' don't follow with: 'But what about the drug baron's nest you're helping to feather?' That's accusatory. Better: 'What's your view on the drug barons?'

The interviewee may want a sympathetic ear just as much as you want revealing answers.

Example You have an appointment with Harry Hunk. Through research you've discovered that both his last two films were on the market as videos within three months of launch.

As you know, the video version of a film is kept under wraps until cinema seat sales start falling. Harry Hunk had the lead in both films. How do you ask him what went wrong?

In a tone that salutes his bravery you say: 'The critics bombed your last two films, but they were obviously both DEPARTURES for you. Would you agree?' Or:

'Maybe the critics misunderstood what you were trying to do. Would you agree?'

Example You have to do a profile on best-selling author Edward Epic. His latest novel, *Dominion*, didn't get rave reviews in the Press as usual, but slithered into oblivion with merely a whisper.

With your antennae alert you know he's expecting praise. If you want a decent interview, all he wants from you is applause – not even sympathy.

You're honest, reasonable, but frank. OK, nobody can produce a winner every time. You have read the book extra carefully. As he's an experienced writer, there's got to be SOME-THING good about it. So when you get round to mentioning *Dominion* say:

'Perhaps it didn't have the impact of your book *Zealot* but what drew me was the characterisation/pace/plot/emotion/dialogue . . .' Just don't mention that the rest was flummadiddle.

Example How do you find out whether the rumoured divorce/pregnancy is true?

If they won't tell you, then they won't. But try wording your question slightly ambiguously SO THEY HAVE A GET OUT. Then they won't feel that you have them pinned against the wall. Going in too direct could startle them into a stony: 'No comment.'

Question 'There seem to be more announcements of divorces than weddings these days. (That gives them prior warning and a few seconds to think.) Did I hear somewhere that you were thinking of severing the knot?'

'First I've heard of it.' Or:

'How did that get out? We only decided last week.'

Question 'Only this week I interviewed a proud dad and two proud mums. There seems to be a lot of it about. Did I hear somewhere that you're knitting baby clothes?'

'Yes – they're for my sister-in-law.' Or:

'Yes – I'm expecting in October.'

Example Athlete Robert Runner suddenly clammed up on you because you asked a probing question. Leave it. Ask the same question later and in a different way. Lean on your creativity here.

You had asked: 'Your first wife. I understand you got divorced after three years?'

'I'd rather not talk about her.'

So you go on to another topic.

But he's had three wives and you get quite a lot about Nos. 2 and 3. Not mentioning No. 1 will look rather incongruous in your write-up.

If he has children by his first wife, much later in the conversation you could ask casually: 'What did their mother do – was she also into sport professionally?'

THE VETO

Sometimes a person will agree to be interviewed only if specific questions are asked and no others. Always agree. At the start of the interview concentrate particularly on establishing friendly rapport and trust. And rigidly avoid the 'no go area'. Later in the meeting, when they've discovered you don't bite (you've worked hard to establish this), you can often find a way of tackling the forbidden.

Example It's rumoured that Gloria Glamour is having an affair with Harry Hunk. But nobody knows for certain. You have an appointment with Ms Glamour, but you only got it on the understanding that there was a veto on mentioning Harry Hunk. So you can't start straight in with: 'How many times have you spent the night with Mr Hunk?'

You start off with: 'What I'd particularly like to know about your next picture is how you REALLY feel about the part. After all, it's a departure from the sex goddess roles you usually play. this is a part any Shakespearian actress would love.'

You let her have her head for much longer than you usually would. Let her agonise about how she's been restricted by her public image – it's not her fault she was born beautiful. (You agree with this.) The directors are at fault, only ever offering her naughty girl parts. (You agree with this too. In fact you actually say: 'Yes, I'll mention that.')

By the time you're three-quarters through the interview Gloria Glamour's formed the opinion that you're a great pal.

(This approach is called diplomacy in the Foreign Office and hypocrisy by the more down to earth.)

Then the Biggy – and you give her the chance of maligning HH: 'I said I wouldn't ask you about Harry Hunk, and I'm not going to press it. But what is it you dislike about him so much that you won't even mention his name?'

GG flutters her eyelashes and says: 'I certainly don't dislike him. Well – I suppose I can tell YOU . . .' and out comes the full story.

· Subtly, subtly. Softly, softly catchee monkey. But you've got to be prepared to spend most of the interview time giving her an ego trip.

Example   Another actress, Deborah Drama, stated categorically that she'd discuss only her career and not her private life.

She had just played the lead in a rather steamy film about soldiers serving abroad, more in danger from the lure and risk of bordellos than the enemy.

After talking about how effective were her director and make-up artist, and how ineffective were the female second lead and cameraman, she'd more or less exhausted the 'career' questions.

I then said: 'I think this is one of the most important films ever made in that it has such a profound message. It reveals that troops on active service aren't involved 24 hours a day in beating hell out of the foe. Much more time is spent in miserable barracks being bored silly.

'Since Attila the Hun, military strategy has been that, when soldiers aren't bashing, they're beering or bonking. And the beer has to run out some time.

'A good many wives, girlfriends and mothers must have been worried by your film. Can you comment on it as a woman, rather than as an actress who took part in it?'

Ms Drama answered: 'Yes, I know more than one woman with a man in the armed forces . . .'

After that I asked her her husband's views – and it progressed from there.

Her current bloke wasn't her husband but a live-in lover (something not generally known). And they had all but fallen out over her provocative and convincing portrayal of a whore.

It brought home to her how far apart they were in some things. This made her give serious thought as to how secure she was if they parted – especially as she had his child. (Oh, really?)

By then Deborah Drama saw me as a soulmate and revealed a great deal about her private life.

Of course, I checked with her that it was OK to mention what she had revealed. And she said 'No'. So I couldn't use it.

But I did interview her a year later and she let me use the facts that she had a child and that (by then) she was estranged from her live-in lover.

OFF THE RECORD

'. . . but he didn't say that in court. And that's off the record, of course.' You've just been given a really juicy fact but the interviewee immediately pours icy water on it. And honourably you must comply.

Journalists are often floored by this. But 'off the record' can work both for and against you.

Your agreement can help the rapport in that the interviewee will feel guilty about the veto and give you other gems of quotes to compensate. And you can always return to that unquotable quote later in the session to see if they've changed their mind now they know you better.

Of course, you can state right at the beginning of the interview: 'Nothing is off the record. If you don't want it printed, then don't tell me.' A great deal depends on how badly you want the interview if you chance this approach. The reaction will be either:

'Oh well, I might as well tell her.' Or:

'OK – no interview.'

Of course, should the information be IMPERATIVE to the write-up, there is a way journalists can sometimes get around the veto. That's when they can find another person who they know witnessed the same event or is a friend of someone who did. When this person is interviewed the hope is that they will tell you what your original interviewee withheld or killed with an 'Off the record'. It's quite legit to get the information from another source.

Then again, it could be YOU who instigates the veto.

The subject says something vicious about another person or lets out an official secret perhaps. You must ask: 'Are you sure you want to say that?'

Do remember there's a law of libel, the Official Secrets Act and a number of other straitjackets. If you fall foul of them you could end up with a hefty fine (that the editor doesn't pay if you're a freelance) and/or a prison sentence.

There's an invaluable book *McNae's Essential Law for Journalists* by Tom Welsh and Walter Greenwood, published by Butterworth's. Read it till you know it's basics off by heart.

But apart from 'Off the Record' statements, you don't have to ask your interviewee's permission to include in your write-up everything else s/he said. Their agreeing to meet you is tantamount to an agreement to this.

PERSONAL GAFFE

However, suppose they tell you something quite personal which you think might embarrass them when it appears in print. Should you ignore it or assume that, as they've told you, they're happy for it to be publicised?

I would always check with them: 'That's a very interesting/ emotive/humorous point – is it OK for me to use this?'

Then you have their 'Yes' on tape, and should they object later, you play them the tape.

CENSORSHIP

As I mentioned earlier in this book, never show your finished piece to the interviewee. Unless s/he's a specialist, in which case sending an editor a technical piece that's been checked is the professional thing to do.

But there is another instance where this comes up – in trade journalism.

The people your editor sends you to interview are usually senior management. They will inevitably ask to see your piece before it's printed.

To these staffers I have to give a different answer from the one I gave to freelances in Chapter 7.

Staffers are in a sticky position in that the people they interview are nearly always the publication's advertisers, or certainly potential advertisers. In other words, the publication's life force. So the journalist is in a cleft stick. S/he may not be able to avoid showing the piece if the interviewee asks.

This is something they have to live with.

BOMBSHELL

What do you do? Your editor sent you to a manufacturer to discuss a new range of electric cookers. When you arrive you're not taken to see the sales manager with whom you have the appointment, but the managing director. He tells you his company are about to take over the country's foremost manufacturer of jet airliners.

This is 'thinking on your feet' time.

There you are without a single question prepared. And you worked so hard researching electric cookers!

First you please the MD by reacting to the Big News favourably: 'That's really great.' Then you play for time. You say: 'I'd really like to focus on that in depth. I know; can we just cover what I originally came for and get that out of the way. Afterwards we'll get on to your Big Story. Then you get two bites of the cherry.'

While you're talking about the cookers, concurrently but on another level of consciousness, you work out a few questions about jet airliners.

And for your initial questions about the new venture, always fall back on the old faithfuls Who, What, Where, Why, When, How. They never fail you.

THE BIG NAME

Don't be intimidated by a gigantic reputation or personality.

Don't be overawed by the Big Name. You're not meeting them as an adoring fan but on a business basis. You are two professionals doing a job of work – and YOU are the one in control. You'll get a far better response from them this way than if you stand there struck paralysed and mute with a mega-dose of hero worship.

Many celebs, especially those in show business, hide behind what is merely a façade built up by their publicity agent. Underneath they are like everybody else – they eat, sleep, moan when they have to get up early, shout at the kids, are afraid of the dentist – just the same as you. What the professional interviewer seeks out is the real person beneath the razzmatazz.

And you could be the eighth interviewer Mr Megastar's seen that week – or even the thirteenth that afternoon – and they all asked predictable questions. Try seeing it through their eyes. They can't be blamed for being short on enthusiasm now it's your turn.

You can easily find out if they've been over-exposed by simply asking: 'Have you given a lot of interviews lately?' Follow that with a genuinely sympathetic: 'That's the unwelcome price of fame, I suppose. What irritates you most about interviewers?' Your comeback to whatever they answer is, of course: 'Oh, that isn't my style. You're going to enjoy this interview. Let's talk about what YOU want. How would you like your public to remember you after you've gone, for instance?' Show them you're on THEIR side, it will help them relax.

Yes, there ARE prima donnas (of both sexes) who think they're God's gift to the Press. If you meet one of these, there's still a human being in there somewhere. Possibly one lacking in confidence who only responds to accolades. It's up to you – COURTEOUSLY – to dig it out, with clever, possibly shock-tactics questioning.

Halfway through you can actually say, beaming a big, sympathetic smile: 'OK, so much for the Big Star. But underneath you're still YOU – and that's the important persona. When was the last time you cried?' And after that: 'Who was your first love and how old were you at the time?' Then perhaps: 'What's your mother's reaction to your fame?'

Let me reassure you, though. Among all the famous people I've interviewed I've met only one prima donna. The big stars who reached the top by being excellent at their jobs are Professionals with a capital P. They don't allow personal temperament to intrude into their interviews with the Press. They know you're there to do a write-up which will benefit them by giving them publicity, so they co-operate.

THE LITTLE NAME

You're doing a profile on an unheard-of concert pianist because he's going to play before the Queen. You're getting a lot of boring or predictable responses. Possibly your interviewee is looking very unhappy about his uninspiring answers.

Try taking a deep breath, digging out the last shred of your enthusiasm and saying: 'Tell me about your typical day – what do you do from waking in the morning to going to bed at night?' Then his typical week, month, year. Then what he'd like to be doing five years from now.

Among that lot there should be at least a few nuggets you stop at and say: 'That's interesting – tell me more.'

NEUROTICS

Any of your interviewees could be neurotic. But don't cross the line between sympathy and empathy. You're not a therapist.

Just a sympathetic smile is usually enough. If you say: 'Tell me about it' and empathise, 'Yes, I've been there too, and what happened to me was XXX', that's getting in far too deep and can take up the rest of the interview. Respect people's phobias and neuroses, but don't join in.

POLITICIANS

More than one student has asked: 'How do you get honest answers from politicians?'

If I knew I could be a millionaire overnight!

MPs are TRAINED to AVOID answering questions. They go on courses where they practise being grilled by experienced interviewers. They're instructed on how to circumnavigate the point of the question – how to box around it plausibly and not commit themselves verbally.

Only journalists looking for a really formidable challenge tackle politicians. Few beginner interviewers have the courage, assertiveness and tenacity. Because politicians are trained to field questions and give non-answers, it's only journalists with a well developed killer instinct who can paint them into a corner.

But you could be in line for the political column of a national newspaper. All you need is a very profound and comprehensive political knowledge and the persistence of Sir Robin Day or Jeremy Paxman.

GONE COLD

What do you do if the interview 'goes cold' on you?

First, how do you know it has?:

(a) they're looking bored/irritated;
(b) they're answering in monosyllables or not answering at all.

Let's say you're focusing on their schooldays perhaps, or marriage to one of the aristocracy. They can have dozens of reasons why they don't want to talk about it. Possibly it was such a non-event in their lives they can't think of anything to say. Or it could have contained a distressing incident (death of a school friend/adultery of spouse) that they're wanting to avoid.

So make it obvious by your body language (sit up straight) and tone of voice (inject more enthusiasm) and say:

'Let's now get on to something completely different' and come in with a shock question along the lines of: 'Tell me how

much you were paid for your last film/book/concert
(whatever).' Or try injecting some humour: 'Everybody has
embarrassing moments, what was your worst one?' or 'What
was the funniest thing that ever happened to you?'

UNINTEREST

You're only a yawn away from falling asleep because your
interviewee is talking about a topic in which you can't raise
even a smidgen of enthusiasm.

Tough. Editors send reporters to interview people on ANY
subject. If the person's speciality doesn't interest you, all the
more reason for really profound research beforehand to discover SOMETHING you can get your teeth into.

And if you're freelancing the same could apply. You're doing
a profile on a celeb – and they launch at length into the delights
of macramé, tennis or fossil hunting, boring the knickers off
you. But some readers will be as keen on this subject as your
celeb is. To them you owe an interesting write-up.

TACITURNITY

How do you coax information out of a taciturn interviewee?

First, WHY are they being unco-operative? If you suspect
they're being deliberately difficult – an ego thing perhaps –
appeal to their vanity/integrity. Let's say you're doing a profile.
You say calmly, but assertively:

'Please forgive me for saying this, but I'm not getting the
information I came for. If I don't have it I can't write the
profile. You were kind enough to agree to being interviewed
and I sense you have a story to tell. Let's look at this problem
or we can't go any further.'

If you suspect your subject is tongue-tied because they're
nervous, use the same words but in a sympathetic tone of
voice.

VERBAL DELUGE

They erupt in an avalanche of words, spewing out information at too great a pace for you to make coherent use of. When they pause for breath (if they don't, then interrupt), say:

'Hey, hold on, hold on. You're a marvellous person to interview – this is all such good stuff I don't want to miss any of it. Let's have a recap. Now, could you repeat what you said about XXX.'

Yes, you're using flattery again – that's one of the interviewer's major strategies, so you'd better get used to it.

And with this Jaw-Me-Dead you'll have to interrupt again – and again probably.

What's worse is meeting an egocentric where the avalanche of words isn't information but claptrap.

The same method applies, except that you'd say: 'Well that's very interesting. But it isn't really what I came to talk about. Perhaps we can return to that later, but now can we get on to my next question, please?' And you'll be OK for a while until they again get the bit between their teeth and you're in for another verbal battering. Some people are just fascinated by the sound of their own voice.

But you can't let them just witter on. Time is finite and you don't want to reach the end of the interview with nothing useable on your tape. You're letting yourself in for hours of transcribing words for which you have no use.

To get your questions answered you have to PERSIST. Try the broken record method. Repeat, and repeat. With this type of person you just have to be firm. Don't ever hesitate to interrupt them (you must be in control).

Tell them: 'As I said before, this is extremely interesting, but if I don't get the answers I came for the editor won't print the piece I write.' That's usually very effective.

And with some people a torrent of words merely means they're ultra-nervous. With them you need to be more gentle.

Let them talk for a couple of minutes. They will soon run out of steam. Then you can say: 'Thank you. I should think I can use some of that. But just so we can be structured, can we now tackle the list of questions I brought.'

But when you say this DO be careful not to use a sarcastic tone. That's a real put-down. And if they're already nervous it could reduce them to a brainless cabbage from whom you'll get nothing but silence and 'I don't know' in response to all your questions.

DIGRESSER

Rather similar to the interviewee with verbal diarrhoea. This one digresses all over the place and away from the point they were making. You need to haul them back with: 'That's very interesting, but could we please get back to XXX.'

LOB IT BACK

Sometimes you will ask your interviewee's opinion on something. They stall by reacting with: 'I'm not sure, what do *you* feel about it?'

Don't follow through. Otherwise you will lose control of the interview. You will have changed roles, and your answering one question can easily lead to others – which use up valuable time. Your editor won't pay you for YOUR replies.

Your response is an amiable grin and: 'I ask the questions – you give the answers.'

SWALLOWERS

Some people have the annoying habit of swallowing their words at the end of each sentence. This isn't a trait they can stop just because you ask them to.

If you meet one of these you need to pay particular attention to the ends of all their important sentences. You then:

(a) scribble a note of the words so you have something to refer to when you transcribe the tape; or

(b) ask them to repeat the words (but you'd be doing this time and time again, so revert to the note-taking).

EXERCISE

You are interviewing Edward Epic whose book *Dominion* was a bit of a dud. His previous books are famous for their gutsy heros, but *Dominion*'s main character was a bit of a nonentity, and he's committed to writing a trilogy.

You want to know:

1 Will Edward Epic try and put more life into the hero in books two and three?
2 If so, how?
3 Or will he drop the idea of a trilogy all together? This will incur the wrath of his publishers who put the words 'First in a blazing trilogy' on the cover of *Dominion*.

Write down how you will word your questions to get this information.

CHAPTER 16

More Problems – Ending the Interview

- Disagreement
- Frauds
- Opposition
- Hostility
- You're not alone
- Bribes

- Questions run out
- Ending
- The Goodbye Trigger
- Reminders
- Exercise.

HERE'S HOW TO COPE with a few more problems. (Nobody said interviewing was easy.)

DISAGREEMENT

Your interviewee disagrees with you. He says X and you know from thorough research, that it's Z. This is embarrassing, especially if he's a specialist of some sort. You will antagonise him if you retort: 'You're wrong.'

The courteous way for you to respond is:

'A lot of people would agree with you on that, but many would dispute it.' Or:

'I'm not so sure Dr Smith would agree with you there; are you sure?' Or:

'That can't be true in all cases, surely?' Or:

'Well that isn't what I heard; could you please qualify that?'

FRAUDS

Perhaps they turn out to be a bit of a fraud. The publicist went overboard in his enthusiasm and told you: 'Apart from writing the longest book ever published, in the same year Samantha Saga also swam the Channel both ways.'

You're chuffed to bits about this. At the interview you bring up the Channel swim. And she's evasive, or puts you off with a glib answer. Don't quit. Don't let this little gem of news get away. Ask her again – ask her to explain. You could discover that she didn't do the Channel at all, she was only training for the swim – which is why she tried to avoid the question.

But salvage as much as you can. To even be training for the event, Ms Saga must be a pretty good swimmer, and you can still put in your profile her recollection of those hours upon tedious hours ploughing up and down the training pool. Perhaps that was when she evolved her plots.

By the way, anything as spectacular as that you should VERIFY. Otherwise you'll have to face the flak if it's later discovered that she can't even swim. Ask her for proof. That sort of swimmer will certainly have certificates for long distances – ask to see them.

The author you interview, Edward Epic, is a racing car enthusiast. He claims he came second in one of the international races.

Ask him for proof. Press cuttings are ideal.

If you suspect him of being a phoney say: 'You seem to have the disadvantage of not being able to prove your statement.' Remember, it's you who'll have egg on your face when the piece is in print and someone questions it. It'll also erode your credibility with the editor.

Be sceptical – always QUESTION statements of fact.

OPPOSITION

What do you do if at the meeting you discover you and your subject are on opposite sides of the fence politically, religiously, racially, whatever?

You stand aside from your own opinions. Professional reporters write OBJECTIVE pieces. Until you reach the status of Bernard Levin your role as a beginner interviewer is not to offer a personal challenge developing into verbal fisticuffs. You're there to get as good a story as possible for several thousand readers who may or may not share the interviewee's views. They're not interested in your private vendetta.

The exception, of course, is if you are a staffer on a strongly biased newspaper. They you have to follow the editorial line.

Yes, yes, I've heard of Lynn Barber *et al.* But I doubt whether that feisty journalist's very first interviews were as controversial as those which have given them a reputation today.

I'm not at all saying 'don't be tough'. I'm merely warning 'first learn your craft'.

HOSTILITY

Your interviewee is aggressive, and shows it.

This could be for so many different reasons:

- they're not feeling well;
- you're the seventh person that week who's put them in the hot seat;
- their shares have fallen;
- they can't tolerate the colour of your sweater;
- they've just got the sack/been made redundant;
- success has gone to their heads;
- a loved one has died;
- they're a bloody-minded Neanderthal.

Nobody has to put up with rudeness. You can merely get to your feet and walk out.

But if this interview is vital, otherwise you can't write your piece – DON'T QUARREL with him/her. If they're name-calling or swearing, DON'T RETALIATE.

It's not easy, but maintain your professionalism. Ignore their abuse, take a very deep breath with your eyes closed, and in a cool, quiet voice change the subject by asking your next question. Some people by their very natures love a fight every now and then – it gives them a buzz. But let them pick someone else. When they see you're not picking up the gauntlet they could very well calm down and behave reasonably.

If you retaliate and have a slanging match you emerge without the information you came for, so you'll be the loser.

YOU'RE NOT ALONE

Interviewing with a third person present (or even more) can be very off-putting. Before you insist on being alone with your subject, a great deal depends on WHY the extra person is there.

If they're merely curious or busy-bodying you can get rid of them with: 'Sorry, but I don't interview with other people in the room.' And you then stand there quietly until they realise you're the one in control, and they leave.

But you're stuck with them if they have a legit reason for being there:

(Interviewee's publicist) 'There are certain clauses in her contract that aren't for the public ear.'

(Her boss) 'There are certain aspects of company policy that cannot be discussed.'

(Her business partner) 'She concentrates on the production, I look after the financial side. You need both of us for a complete picture of our operation.'

(Her other half) 'She needs my support, she's never faced the Press alone.'

(Her mother) 'She's just getting over a nervous breakdown.'

(Her kids) 'My babysitter couldn't make it, I've nowhere else to leave them.'

The only advice is, try to ignore them.

If the third person keeps interrupting, tell them: 'Look, I'm sorry, but I came to get details from X (your original interviewee). It's her I want to talk to, nobody else. Otherwise the editor won't print my write-up.'

BRIBES

Money or gifts have no place in an interview. You don't pay them and they don't pay you.

If they ask for a fee tell them firmly that you never pay. As a beginner you're not into cheque-book journalism.

If they insist AND THE INTERVIEW IS VITAL TO YOU, tell them you'll check with the editor. Say: 'It's not my responsibility.' Editors don't like to pay, but a national newspaper will occasionally if it's a really BIG story and an exclusive. If the editor agrees, don't forget to get a RECEIPT. You claim it on expenses and this is your only proof.

If you interview them over a drink or a meal – even a modest cup of coffee – ethics dictate that YOU pay for it. You also always offer to pay their travel expenses. It's ethical – it's also part of being in control. If they pay you are immediately beholden and this jeopardises you writing completely objectively.

It's the old Freedom of the Press. Ethical journalists can't be bought.

QUESTIONS RUN OUT

You've booked an hour with a Big Name and three-quarters of the way through you run out of the questions you've prepared. You're sitting there and there's a horrible silence while your subject looks at you expectantly.

Look at the notes you've been taking (as well as using a tape recorder). Do it calmly, say: 'I'd like to recap now.' Don't look flustered or you'll lose control.

Have a good think back over what s/he's already told you. There will have been a number of points you can RETURN to.

'Can we go back to the people you met: (actor) at the academy where you were a student; (author) during the research you did in Acapulco; (rock singer) on your first tour?'

And there will be other points your subject has made that you can ask them to expand upon.

Three other questions with lengthy answers:

- What's the attitude of your family to your job/hobby/cause?
- What advice would you give to a school leaver wanting to do what you do?
- If you could have your life over again would you tread the same career path?

And whatever the answer, you follow with: 'Why?' or 'Why not?'

ENDING

It is courteous to let your subject know when you're ending the interview. YOU are the one with the list of questions, and YOU are the one with your watch on the table.

1   Do a mental check that you've enough answers to make a decent length write-up. Otherwise do what I suggested above, recap on some of the points made. Check that you've UNDER-STOOD all that's been said. It's very amateur to have to ring afterwards to ask.

2   Your subject might have something valuable to add and hasn't seen an opportunity to mention it. If you suddenly leap to your feet saying: 'Right. That's it. Goodbye', he won't be brave enough to bring it up.

The simplest and most natural way to warn him is: 'One last question, Mr Smith . . .' and after his reply, follow up with: 'Is there anything I haven't mentioned that you think is important?'

3   Remember, it's a good idea to part amicably – you might want to interview this person again because:

(a) There's a big deal. In three months it falls through, so you need another interview.
(b) Samantha Saga will have another book next year which you'd like to talk about.

(c) He's an up and coming athlete; at the next Olympic Games he wins a Gold, and you're the one who interviews him.

(d) You've got to be able to look them in the eye when you accidentally bump into them on the railway station AFTER they've read what you've written.

4 If you were courteous and considerate all the way through, then, when you wind down the session, they're not thinking 'Thank God it's over' but 'I admit, I actually enjoyed that.'

5 So when you've finished questioning, turn off the machine, stand up and, with a smile, shake hands. Say something like: 'Thanks, I seem to have all the information I need. You've given me some really interesting stuff. I wish all my interviews were like this.'

THE GOODBYE TRIGGER

Sometimes, as your interviewee escorts you to the door, s/he comes out with a little gem of an anecdote that will 'make' your profile/feature.

It's happened to me, more than once. And strangely enough I know it has happened to several doctors in a slightly different context.

One GP pal told me a man in his 50s came to see him complaining about backache. Have you walked into a door or fallen, done any gardening recently or shifted any furniture? No to all of those.

My friend prescribed an analgesic cream to rub on and advised him to take it easy.

On the way out, pulling on his gloves, the patient remarked that he must remember to buy some tough workmen's gloves as he'd cut his hand on a piece of jagged metal yesterday.

'How did you do that?'

'Well I'm helping this old lady clear out her cellar. She had a bit of old coal she didn't want. I put it in bags for the Sally Ann.'

'Was there much coal?'

'No – only a few bags full – about five or six hundredweight I'd reckon.'

And there you had the cause of the backache. The macho patient had considered coal moving too trivial an activity to mention to the doctor.

And likewise with people you interview.

When the worry of the face-to-face confrontation is over, they lapse back into their 'normal self'. Then they may tell you a home truth which they had been deliberately or inadvertently neglecting when you were feeling around the topic earlier. They subconsciously think this is 'off the record' time. But you don't. After you've left you industriously jot it all down in your notebook before you forget. I've often done this in the interviewee's loo!

REMINDERS

At the end of the interview is a good time to remind them about the photo they mentioned – and any dates they said they'd look up for you.

EXERCISE

Your interviewee has stopped mid-sentence, halfway through an account of how he got a film director fired.

He says: 'I'm not going any further for free. If you want any more you've got to pay for it.'

Write down what you'd say WITHOUT RE-READING this chapter.

CHAPTER 17

Transcription

- Transcribe soon
- Short write-up
- 500 words upwards
- No full stops!
- Highlighter
- Contradictions
- Warts an' all

- Two professional opinions
- Sensationalism
- Verify doubtfuls
- Libel
- Store tapes
- Exercise.

TRANSCRIBE the tape with as little delay as possible. Try not to let it 'go cold' on you. It might not be convenient to WRITE the piece straight away, but early transcription has two advantages:

(a) You might discover that the tape isn't clear in places, so the SOONER you transcribe it the more you will remember of what was said. For instance, your subject may have started sentences but not finished them.

(b) You can get down on paper your initial reactions to comments the interviewee made. For instance you might suspect the subject was unsure of his facts or even lying in places.

This may not be apparent in the actual words he used, but your gut feeling at the time was disbelief. So you'll type in [?] to remind yourself to check that fact at another source, or leave it out all together. Professional journalists have a rule: IF IN DOUBT, LEAVE IT OUT.

Your gut reactions are an integral part of the really creative process. It's YOUR mental responses to words spoken that are exclusive to you and what make it obvious that the final write-up comes from YOUR pen. It's an important source of personal style. So make a note to check out any doubts you have.

I prefer to use public transport when I leave an interview rather than drive because I can make notes on the way home. And it's then, immediately after the interview, that I often think of an ideal and impactful opening for the piece I'm going to write.

My transcripts are dotted with words in brackets which are notes to me – not only lies, but other statements will need checking like statistics and possibly dates – just type [check] after their words. Then you can expand the ideas fully and correctly when you come to actually writing the feature or profile.

SHORT WRITE-UP

If you're writing a feature and you're interviewing a number of people, you won't need yards and yards of transcript from any one person. Perhaps you will need only a couple of quotes from the interview.

The fastest way to tackle this is:

(a) Listen to it all the way through noting the exact position (the number on the tape counter) of the words you want to use.

(b) Rewind, then Fast Forward to each quote you want to type out.

500 WORDS UPWARDS

Be prepared to put aside a decent amount of TIME for transcription. A mere one-hour interview can take about five hours to transcribe from the tape to the typewriter or word processor. A great time-saver is a foot-pedal-operated machine as this will leave your hands free for typing.

As you'll need to scribble notes all over your transcript, it's a good idea to type it in double line spacing.

The finished transcript can be a bit daunting. An hour's interview can result in perhaps 15 pages, something like 4,500 words. All this for a write-up that will possibly be only 500 words.

As a beginner, transcribe the tape pretty fully. You can bet that if you deliberately leave out some seemingly uninteresting passage, it'll be just that one that's needed to make sense of an important statement that comes later on the tape.

What you CAN leave out is all but the bare bones of the questions YOU ask. You can also ignore all the interviewee's 'ums', 'ers', 'you knows' and 'actuallys'.

NO FULL STOPS

When you sit in front of your word processor and start running your tape, THAT'S when it comes home to you that people don't speak in nice tidy sentences with full-stops and commas in all the right places. Neither do people speak grammatically – the spoken word is always colloquial.

SO HOW MUCH LICENCE DO YOU HAVE TO EDIT?

There's nothing wrong with SLIGHT amendments to give the comments a better 'flow', correct grammar or cut non-essential wordage. What you mustn't do is alter the ESSENCE or the SENSE of what was said. This for two reasons:

• If the tape was called into court and you misrepresented the interviewee, the offence is prosecutable.
• You will lose the unique 'voice' of the individual, their 'personality'.

Example (From an actual interview with an author whose first novel shot straight into the best-seller list.)

Q   How did you learn about how well the sales were doing?
A   Actually Dorabella rang me – my publisher – Dorabella's my publisher – I mean it was fantastic – when she told me I literally died.

[The next comment should be: Well, this is fascinating, I've never interviewed a corpse before! In the write-up it came out as: 'My publisher rang me. It was fantastic, I nearly died.']

Q So did you celebrate?
A Of course – I can't – yes I can – I remember – THAT was the excuse for the car. I bought a car – a new one – this year's model.
[In the write-up: 'I bought a car, this year's model.']

Q When did you buy it, straight away?
A I went down to the showroom – on a Wednesday. No wait – it was a Thursday – my wife was with me, actually. Hang about, it was last week. I saw a smashing car, you know.
['I bought it last week.']

Q Would you say you bought it on impulse?
A Well I think I want – because, er – it was hot on that day – very hot – Mediterranean sun like. Oh, I should explain, it was an open top – a dream. Impulsive? Yeah, well I suppose I am a bit – I have to admit – I do sometimes. I'm literally a creature of impulse.
['It was an open-top dream – I bought it because it was a hot day. I'm literally a creature of impulse.']

HIGHLIGHTER

Despite your well-organised questioning, the interviewee doesn't always tell you everything about a topic, then go on to the next one.

No, a third of the way through topic 'F' they return to 'A', then wash in a bit of 'N' that you haven't asked them yet and would prefer they didn't mention out of the chronological order of your questions. And so it all becomes a bit of a mishmash.

This is where highlighter pens are invaluable. You go through the typescript and pick out all the bits about the first marriage in pink, the second marriage in blue, the career in green, the nervous breakdown in mauve – and so on.

A colleague of mine goes even further – he had the walls of his study faced with cork. He reads through the transcript and counts the number of major points he wants to use in his write-up; then gets that number of photocopies.

He then cuts out all the references to childhood and puts them in one pile, another about building the house in Alberta in another pile, about the bankruptcy trauma in another and yet another of the comeback after six years.

Then, taking a pile of cuttings he pastes them on to a sheet of continuous print-out paper in logical sequence, and pins the sheet on the wall. He does this with each pile, but he hasn't finished yet.

He goes around the room with three highlighters. All the 'extremely good' quotes he highlights in blue, the 'good' ones in pink and the 'fair' ones in yellow.

Then, when he gets down to the actual writing, he doesn't have to search for the best quotes as they're all there ready. He can rattle off a 2,000-word profile in a morning.

And the fact that he has to keep getting up to look at the wall is a bonus, he says, as being a journalist is such a sedentary job and it gives him much needed exercise.

Yet another highlighter help. An hour-long interview should yield enough comments for more than one write-up. Think up your markets – a total of three, perhaps. The blue highlighter is for quotes you'll use for a profile for *NME*, say, pink for another for *GQ* and green for a very short one in *Take-A-Break*.

CONTRADICTIONS

There are two types of contradiction – factual and human.
1   Factual – these need checking so you can use the correct one.

Example 'I understand you come from a talented Irish family with a great theatrical tradition. How many children did your grandmother have?'
'Twelve that lived.'
'And they all went into show business?'

'Yes. Including my mother there were five girls – they had a dancing/singing act called the Five Belles. The six boys danced and sang too but all went their individual ways. Most of them ended up in the chorus of one of the opera houses.'

2   Human – these are a delight and do a great deal to illustrate the personality of your interviewer.

Example   'How methodical a writer are you?'

'Not at all. I'm still only halfway through my novels about two weeks before the deadline. I'm a shambolic worker.'

'So you don't have a meticulous structure?'

'Oh yes – always.'

'Then you *are* a methodical writer?'

'Yes – I have to have all my research carefully labelled and filed before I can even start.'

WARTS AN' ALL

It's seldom your remit to present your subject warts an' all. If they're a particularly swollen-headed, belligerent type you can sometimes take them down a peg or two by quoting them verbatim. But if not, don't let your subject appear illiterate or ridiculous.

Example 1   'The critics seemed to agree that your last film bombed. How do you feel about it?'

'Well it ain't my fault – it was the friggin director wot cocked it up.'

In the write-up I would put: 'Well it wasn't my fault, it was the director's.'

And if the person drops all their 'Hs', you wouldn't write the words without initial 'Hs'. Be kind – they were kind enough to grant you the interview.

Grammar – if it's incorrect, always tidy it up. Unless, of course, your subject deliberately uses bad grammar in a humorous context, such as 'English as she is spoke.'

Example 2   It's not unusual, when an interviewee is a little nervous, for him to use a word he wouldn't in normal conversation. And it's up to you not to make him look ludicrous, but to change it.

(a) 'My latest book is the first in a serious.' You'd write 'series'.

(b) 'I rang, and rang, and rang all week but couldn't get an answer. Then on Friday he finally deemed to speak to me.' You'd write 'deigned'.

TWO PROFESSIONAL OPINIONS

Freelance journalist John Diamond says: 'It's tempting to quote what you'd like someone to say, or what you think they meant to say. Don't. Write what they do say.'

Unless a subject's inarticulacy is germane to the pieces, there's no need to draw attention to it. There's nothing wrong with tidying up a quote for public consumption.

Mike Virgo, editor of *Stationery Trade Review* says: 'There isn't a local councillor or politician who hasn't been grateful to some journalist for reporting what they MEANT to say, instead of what they DID say.

'But there are two rules on this. What you write must be an EXACT paraphrase of what they said. And the other – and the journalist must have a sixth sense about this – don't put into their mouth words that are out of their character, words they wouldn't normally use.'

SENSATIONALISM

Don't get too carried away – not as much as this tyro who interviewed Edward Epic, and heard him say:

'My eleven-year-old fell out of our little apple tree and broke her ankle. As with any father, it was a pretty intense situation when she was taken to hospital – but thankfully it was nothing serious.'

Our beginner journalist seizes on the word 'intense' and peps up the profile with:

'Agonised with grief, Edward Epic kept vigil by the hospital bed while his baby girl was in intensive care.' (Ouch!)

VERIFY DOUBTFULS

Do remember to verify comments that are a bit larger than life, e.g. your interviewee tells you that he was mugged by three men but he retaliated and put all three of them in hospital.

Be a trifle sceptical. It's better to be brave at the time and ask: 'Three? That's incredible. Please don't mind my questioning this but my write-up has to be factual. Did you REALLY put three thugs in hospital?'

LIBEL

Some quotes you deliberately don't write up. If your interviewee slanders someone, leave it out. OK, it might be a juicy bit of reader-grabbing gossip – but if you write it down it becomes libel.

It is punishable libel even if:

(a) what was written WAS SAID;
(b) what was said WAS TRUE.

The law of libel decrees that it's the EFFECT the written statement has on the victim that is at issue, not what was said.

It is also indictable to LEAVE OUT PARTS OF WHAT WAS SAID, if this alters the meaning of the statement.

Example 'I went to bed with Peter's wife (before she was married to him).' This entire sentence was what was actually said. You can't leave out the words in brackets.

Example The reporter wrote: 'Smith admitted to having visited the building on the day the fire broke out. When he was asked if he was carrying combustible fuel he said: "Yes".'

The transcript:

'Did you visit the building on the day it was gutted by fire?'
'Yes.'
'Were you carrying petrol?'
'Yes' (nervous laugh), 'but only in my cigarette lighter.'

An 'accurate' report, of course – and the editor loved it, (or he would have done if this had been a genuine interview). If the entire quote had been written, it would have killed the story stone dead.

The WRITER is liable for libel – prison sentences and fines are heavy – and editors don't pay freelance journalists' fines. There's more about libel in *The Writers' & Artists' Yearbook* and much more in *McNae's Essential Law for Journalists* by Tom Welsh and Walter Greenwood (Butterworths).

STORE TAPES

Always keep ALL your tapes and notebooks for at least five years. Misrepresentation and libel cases take forever to get into the court system. Your tape may be your only means of defence (see Chapter 12).

EXERCISE

Without re-reading this chapter, name the two advantages of transcribing your tape immediately you can get to your WP/typewriter, rather than leave it till later?

CHAPTER 18

Transcript and Write-up

Here is a transcript of an interview by Stan Nicholls, and the profile of Joan Clayton that was written from it. Stan Nicholls, a very experienced journalist, author and tutor is a guest speaker on the author's journalism courses. This ten-minute interview was done in class as a demonstration.

This example shows what a raw transcript looks like and the fact that it's three times the length (1,500 words) of the write-up, which was a stipulated 500 words. The average interview of one hour has a transcript five times this length, of course.

You can see the exact questions asked – many of them open-ended – as well as the answers, with all the warts left in.

I have also chosen this example because it's about a beginner journalist and it gives useful information on the start of a journalistic career.

STAN   I know you've had a number of different jobs, but for the purpose of this interview I'd like to concentrate on one career – as an editor. What kind of things did you edit?

JOAN   Industrial publications and trade publications.

S   Those are rather specialised fields – how did you get into these areas?

J   I started, as many journalists do, as an editorial assistant. I remember there were just the editor and I running the publication – a glossy monthly. But – well – my real training as an editor started on the day my editor's wife rang to say her husband was in hospital in a meningitis coma, and he was liable to be away for quite some time. Well – I was terrified.

S It was down to you to take over and get the publication out?

J Yes, I mean I'd only been there about seven months. It was the official journal of a trade association and there was nobody to get it out except me. I had to write most of it – only a couple of contributions from outsiders.

I DID get it out – not on time, but with lots of crying and swearing and praying and sleeping at the office I got the thing out about a fortnight late. If it hadn't been for . . . I had to lean heavily on the printer – he was an enormous help.

My editor didn't come back for six months – I brought out five other editions gradually getting closer and closer to the scheduled deadline, till the later editions were coming out on time.

S So he came back eventually – but this must have been a slightly awkward situation because you'd kind of taken a step up professionally, hadn't you? How did you proceed from there?

J I stayed there for a few months then I was head-hunted would you believe – IPC Business Press, part of the *Daily Mirror* Group. They publish several hundred trade journals.

S IPC's a really big company. Presumably you got a really good training?

J Not at all – not a damn thing – well I wasn't offered anything. I wasn't aware that there was any formal in-house or external training for us plebs – we're talking about the early seventies now. My sub merely chucked back my write-ups in stony silence. As I was too scared to ask what was wrong with them, I just kept rewriting till he kept them.

In those days it was a closed shop. For sheer survival all the journalists needed to belong to the NUJ and the layout artists to SLADE. But I don't remember any training. Today, of course, the NUJ has a vast programme of structured training for newcomers.

S You surprise me – you say you didn't learn anything at all with IPC?

J   Oh no – I learnt an enormous amount. Imagine a building, perhaps the size of this college, with dozens of trade journals in it, each with its own suite of offices. I gradually got to know the journals either side of our suite. I was on a tabloid for the stationery and office equipment trade, our neighbours were architecture and pop music – *Melody Maker* I think it was.

    I went around picking up tips – page layout – I learned how to be a graphics artist by watching the artists making up pages and by picking their brains. I was the features editor on my journal and I started designing all the feature pages myself.

S   How long were you with IPC?

J   Oh I don't know – let's see – years – can't remember . . .

S   Where did you go after IPC?

J   I think it's inherent in many, many journalists that they would like to sit in the editor's chair, even to launch a publication, to create it from nothing.

    So I looked around for editorships in the Trade Press, couldn't find any I liked the sound of, so started to look in the Industrial Press. I found an ad for an aluminium company – they wanted an editor to launch a tabloid newspaper, so I took it.

S   You mention both Trade and Industrial journalism – presumably the same principles apply to both?

J   Identical. Whatever brand of journalism you're in it's always the same basic tenets.

S   This aluminium industry job was your first as a full-blown editor?

J   Yes.

S   How many staff did you have?

J   Only a secretary – did all the interviewing, writing and page layout myself.

S   How long did you stay?

J   Eighteen months.

S   Wasn't very long.

J   Well between them, this company's workforce of only 900 belonged to 14 different unions. The shop stewards wouldn't allow any information to go directly from manage-

ment to employees. It all had to be disseminated by them.
The reason I was brought in was to launch a tabloid newspaper carrying news of what was going on in the company,
the readers being the employees.

Well, the shop stewards banned my paper. They didn't
want it to go to the workforce – I found it burnt in the yard.
After 18 months of banning my paper I thought 'nuts to
this' and . . .

S   Hang on, you're a member of a union yourself.

J   I wouldn't have been able to work for the company unless
I belonged to a union. But the NUJ weren't recognised
by the company, they weren't one of the 14 with whom
negotiations were made.

S   So how did this situation resolve itself?

J   Afraid the company had to close down – unions killed the
golden goose. I was part of an industrial relations move to
try and repair inter-company relations that were hide-
bound by continuous strikes, but it failed.

S   So you left – it must have been very depressing.

J   Oh – well – yes – I was very unhappy.

S   So what did you do after that?

J   Looked around for another job in the same industry because
I knew a bit about aluminium by then, but couldn't find one.
Then I saw a particularly interesting ad for an editor to launch
a whole series of publications and closed circuit TV programmes for a pharmaceuticals company – so I took that.

S   More industrial journalism?

J   Yes. I liked the look of this job very, very much – I was
entirely autonomous, something I got into my contract of
employment. I reported directly to the managing director –
not even other board directors had any jurisdiction over
me – stayed there several years.

S   You had some staff?

J   A secretary, an editorial assistant and an assistant editor –
plus a regular stable of freelance writers and photographers
and cartoonists.

S   This might be a good point to ask you what the function of an
editor in industry is. Can you give me a typical rota of duties?

J   Go around the shop floor, laboratories and offices interviewing – asking what was going on in their neck of the woods, what was their current project, what was new.

S I understand you got a national award while you were with that company?

J Er yes – well – yes, during the many years I was with them I launched a tabloid newspaper, a newsmagazine, a satirical magazine, CTV news/magazine programmes and an annual financial report for employees. It was the report that won the award – a very new concept in the early 80s – the company report was something the shareholders got but the employees, who made the whole thing possible in the first place, weren't given any information on the company's turnover.

S Who gave the awards?

J BAIA – no E – BAIE, the British Association of Industrial Editors.

S And you got it three years running, I believe?

J Er – well yes . . .

S I know you've used your experiences as an editor and journalist as a basis for other projects – tutoring this course, for instance. And something else – you've written a couple of books on journalism, haven't you?

J Heck . . . those, well – yes, there's *Interviewing for Journalists* which is a sequel to *Journalism for Beginners*. They're both based on courses I run here – and questions asked by students.

S And isn't the first one on London University's reading list for their extra-mural journalism course?

J Yes – I was told it is.

S Is it possible to design and edit trade or industrial publications as a freelance?

J Oh yes – I was eventually made redundant from the pharmaceuticals company. Then I went freelance and made a great deal more money as a freelance editor than I could as a staffer – launched a newspaper for another pharmaceutical company, as well as working for other companies in oil, and fields like tourism, severely disabled people and management consultancy.

S How easy is it to get into freelance editorship?

J   Well – well if you have a great deal of experience it's not difficult. I was twenty years on the payrolls of the companies I've told you about where I learned how to put a journal together, cope with printers, with freelance contributors, with the many contingencies. I suppose you've got to be a good organiser – assertive – you need a very thorough, all round experience to become an editor.

S   Is trade and industrial journalism an area you'd recommend new journalists to try?

J   Certainly. I would do it all again – I got 200 per cent job satisfaction.

END OF INTERVIEW

The following profile had an editorial restriction to 500 words. It shows how to let the quotes tell the story – there's a minimum of narrative. It was written by one of my students.

'I get 200 per cent job satisfaction,' says editor Joan Clayton, who won a national award despite having had no formal training and one of her publications burned.

The award, which she got three years running, was given by the British Assoc. of Industrial Editors. It was for an annual financial report for staff – a new concept in the early eighties. 'The company report was something the shareholders got, but the employees – who made the whole thing possible – weren't given any information on the company's turnover.'

And subsequently, Ms Clayton has had a couple of books published – *Journalism for Beginners* and *Interviewing for Journalists*. The first book is on the recommended reading list for London University extra-mural students of journalism.

These aren't the results of extensive formalised training but a pretty ad hoc, DIY method.

Joan Clayton started in one of the traditional ways, as an editorial assistant. 'My real training as an editor started on the day my editor's wife rang to say her husband was in hospital in a meningitis coma.

'I'd only been there about seven months. It was the official journal of a trade association and there was nobody to get it out but me.

'With lots of crying and swearing and praying and sleeping at the office I got the thing out about a fortnight late.'

She was later head-hunted by IPC Business Press – and did she get some good training here?

'Not a damn thing. There seems to have been no formal in-house or external training – we're talking about the early seventies now. The sub merely chucked back my write-ups in stony silence. As I was too scared to ask what was wrong with them, I just kept re-writing till he kept them.

'In those days it was a closed shop. For sheer survival journalists needed to belong to the NUJ. But I don't remember any training. Today, of course, the NUJ has a vast programme of structured training for newcomers.'

Didn't she learn anything while with IPC Business Press?

'I learnt an enormous amount. I was on a tabloid for the stationery and office equipment trade. I went around picking up tips on page layout and learned how to be a graphics artist by watching the artists making up pages.'

So with a solid grounding in newspaper editorial and design she eventually took a job in industrial journalism as an editor.

But the job lasted only eighteen months.

'The shop stewards wouldn't allow information to go directly from management to employees. So they banned my tabloid – I found it burnt in the yard.'

So she moved on – to a pharmaceuticals company.

'Yes, I liked this job very much, I was entirely autonomous. During my many years with this company I launched a tabloid newspaper, a newsmagazine, a satirical magazine, CTV news/magazine programmes and an annual financial report for staff. It was the report that won the award.'

· EXERCISE

1 Re-read the transcript.
2 Write your own version, EXACTLY 500 WORDS. In other words, merely re-structure this write-up. Start with a different intro and try a different angle from 'training'.

CHAPTER 19

Writing It Up

- Don't dither
- It needs impact
- Quote marks
- Structure
- Feature analysed

- Spite and Indiscretion
- Intriguing quotes
- Unconscious ridicule
- Marketing tips
- Exercise.

I WANT TO BE FAIR to readers of *Journalism for Beginners* (now in paperback). So unless it is absolutely necessary, I do not repeat here writing tips used in that book. The first book focuses specifically on writing skills, so I assume that readers of this sequel, *Interviewing for Journalists*, can write to professional standard.

DON'T DITHER

There's a valuable axiom: 'Don't get it right, get it written'. In other words don't be fastidious about your first draft, just get the words down on paper. The editing, the titivating, comes in subsequent drafts. What you'll capture in your first draft is SPONTANEITY – which will have dribbled away by the time you come to draft No.2.

IT NEEDS IMPACT

And, unless it comes spontaneously early on, that imperative and vital OPENING WITH IMPACT is something you can worry about later, too. It will need a great deal of thought as it's so important to selling the final piece.

Remember the people you are writing for. Hopefully people who THINK, therefore they will have jobs and/or be running a home and family, so they don't have a great deal of TIME to kill. They seldom read magazines and newspapers from cover to cover, they read only the pieces that catch their eye in the first sentence. Editors know this, that's why pieces without a strong opening are rejected.

As a beginner you haven't got EXPERIENCE to offer to an editor, so sock him in the eye with your intro.

For a PROFILE intro you could use:

- the most dramatic/emotional/humorous thing that happened to your interviewee; or
- their strongest/most controversial quote; or
- a list; or
- acute observation; or
- a question, so the reader will read on to find the answer.

Examples

'The day his son was hit by a car was the worst day of Harry Hunk's life', or 'Harry Hunk never wants to make a Western again. While filming his most recent one he fell off his horse in front of a crowd of adoring fans.'

'There are a number of things which we in this country are good at. One of them is underselling ourselves. It is time we put the "Great" back into Britain,' says Prince Charles. Or 'When men unzip their pants their brains fall out,' says Jackie Collins.

(start with a list) 'Ballet dancer, ski instructor, swimming coach and radiographer were all experimental career steps before Edward Epic settled on surviving by his pen. He has used all these experiences in his novels to create authentic backgrounds and profound insights into the characters.'

'Robert Maxwell died above the fold' (by Mark Frankel with Jennifer Foote, *Newsweek*), or 'The only silent thing about

American writer Camille Paglia is the third letter of her second name. This is a woman whose publicist calls to warn you to bring a tape-recorder to the interview because even the most accomplished shorthand writer cannot hope to keep up' (by Leslie White, *Sunday Times*).

'Why does Samantha Saga want to spend six months working as a vet's assistant?' or 'How many careers did Robert Runner have before he became a professional athlete?'

Some editors don't like a quote at the beginning because it creates a type-setting difficulty. Just take a look at your nearest newspaper or magazine; you'll see that most printed pieces start with what's known as a 'dropped cap' – an initial capital letter that's much larger than the rest of the word, so takes up space in the line(s) below the first one. Starting with a quote means starting with quote marks and they look slightly odd floating in space to the left of the big cap.

But design should be the servant of communication, not its master. Ring your target publication and ask if they veto quote openings.

The first sentence of the write-up often occurs to you at the interview. Your subject makes a comment and you underline it in your notebook 'GREAT INTRO'.

You also need an impactful beginning for a FEATURE:

Examples

'Hurlingham, London's most prestigious members' sports club, is under siege from a pea-green bunker that has arisen in the pit of the old Fulham power station. It is threatening to lure younger members away with a mixture of Eighties kudos and state-of-the-art chic' (by Sophie Laybourne, *London Evening Standard*).

'No one could be unchanged after almost a month on the desert frontline of Saudi Arabia, in the company of some of the world's bravest war reporters – Colin Smith *The Observer*, Jon Swain *The Sunday Times/The Killing Fields*, Robert Fisk

The Independent, Charlie Glass ex-Beirut hostage, ABC Television and *The Spectator et al.*' (by Simon Freeman, *Mirabella*).

QUOTE MARKS

I shouldn't think you'll need reminding about the uses of double and single quotes (inverted commas) – but I will. The rule is: in newspapers, singles come inside doubles to indicate (a) that another person is talking, (b) a title or unusual phrase/word. In books (like this one) the rule may be reversed. Find out the preferred style of the publication you're writing for and follow it scrupulously.

Examples

After the match Gareth Goalie was delirious with joy: 'That's our fifteenth win this season. Larry's prophesy is coming true. He told me in the changing room: "We'll make Wembley this year, see if we don't." And if we go on like this, we will.'

My student, Bryan, said: 'I think Ann Hoffmann's book "Research for Writers" is tremendously helpful.'

John asked: 'Do you reckon Dr Smith's system of "method thinking" is any good?'

If it's a long enough comment to need more than one paragraph, you re-start the paragraph with quotes BUT you don't end the previous one with them. Save the final set of quotes till the end of the comment.

Example (Following an announcement that several coal mines were to close.)

In a letter to *The Independent* the Bishop of Southwark, the Rt Rev Roy Williamson, questioned 'the morality of such a cavalier destruction of thousands of lives.

'It is not only poor reward for an industry that in recent years has responded superbly to productivity targets, it is also a sad reflection on the Government's ability to keep its promises.

'It will have a demoralising effect on the whole nation.'

STRUCTURE

Students ask me for a formula they can follow to structure the writing of profiles, news features and news stories. The nearest I can give you to a formula is Who, What, Where, When, Why, How.

These six essential factors have to be included for the piece to be professional and successful. It is quite immaterial in which order they appear, it's just that the piece is incomplete if any one of them is absent.

This rule of thumb applies implicitly to news features and news stories. For profiles, you still need those six factors to make the piece complete.

But, of course, there are several styles of profiles:

1 Q&A (Question and Answer); or
2 Feature.

And both of these can be either:

(a) Holistic (entire life); or
(b) Specific (one incident, perhaps a book launch).

Decide which one you're tackling before you do the interview.

The Q&A format is a gift for the beginner journalist. Not having any narrative, it's easiest to write. If you feel you want to tackle this format first then hunt down magazines that use it. If X magazine's spot 'Face of the Week' is in Q&A format in the editions you read, you can rely on the fact that this is the way they want it each time.

In a profile, aim to present facets of your interviewee that have not yet been discovered. For instance, what has fame done to them? Is their 'public' persona different from their 'private' one?

FEATURE ANALYSED

Here's a 1,500 word feature analysed according to the gospel of WWWWWH. It appeared in *Office Lifestyle* and was written by Janet Taylor who has kindly given me her permission to reproduce it.

It is cleverly structured. Note first its intro with a great deal of impact which is extended by examples of specific disasters. These end with the explosion at Commercial Union, which leads naturally into outlining help available. The beginning plays on the emotions of all office management – 'Hell! This could happen to me!' Then, cleverly building up, it altruistically points out that help is at hand.

When the WHAT (the help) is introduced, the reader is looking for it, and it gets their full attention.

IF DISASTER STRIKES – WILL YOU BE READY?

If a terrorist bomb destroyed your head office tomorrow, could you offer business as usual by Monday? Or what if a blackmailer laced your food products with poison, or a spillage from one of your manufacturing plants threatened to cause an environmental catastrophe, or the chief executive went missing . . . how would your company cope?

If you have never given any of those prospects serious thought, then you are not alone. Surveys reveal that the vast majority of companies have no idea how they would respond to a disaster. If anything happened, they would just play it by ear.

Yet the midst of a crisis is surely no time to be making fundamental decisions, especially when the strategies adopted, necessarily in haste, can make or break the business.

Crisis management is a recent management issue that has arisen in response to the well-publicised catastrophes that have occurred of late.

Among those deemed to have been badly handled, the King's Cross fire and Bhopal toxic leak are probably the most harrowing. However, Perrier can possibly provide as good an example as any of how to make a bad situation worse. Their advertising slogan in the States – 'It's Perrier – it's perfect' – came back to haunt them when a technical failure at a plant in France caused the company to withdraw 160 million bottles world-wide. Minute traces of benzene had been identified in the water.

The level of public concern was heightened by the company's failure to brief the Press effectively at the time of the scare and, subsequently, to reassure the public that the problem had been eliminated. To make matters worse, Perrier was not insured for product recall costs.

The company has since been taken over by Nestlé.

In contrast, other firms have emerged from disaster with their reputations enhanced. For example Johnson and Johnson in the States were widely praised for the way they handled the lacing of their Tylenol capsules with cyanide.

And, living up to their advertising slogan of not making a drama out of a crisis, Commercial Union managed to turn their disaster into a triumph.

During the evening of Friday, April 10, 1992, an explosion in the City of London devastated CU's head office. Before the night was out, the pre-determined disaster plan had been activated.

Over that weekend, telephone and computer links were reinstated, alternative accommodation had been set up for the 650 head office staff – and they had all been informed – and the Press had been fully briefed. On Monday morning, advertisements were appearing in national newspapers confirming that it was 'business as usual'.

It was a staggering achievement and people were impressed indeed, according to John Athawes, marketing development manager of Commercial Union Risk Management: 'A marketing benefit was obtained from a potentially disastrous situation, due to positive publicity, and clear evidence of effective pre-planning.'

An independent offshoot of Commercial Union, CURM can help with the setting up of an overall plan for concerns which wish to anticipate, and thereby minimise, the consequences of disaster. Other companies have introduced more specific packages. Blue Line, for example, are offering to maintain stocks of desks, chairs and storage units as scheduled by a customer, and deliver them within 24 hours of notification that they are needed.

Designed to be self-financing, the scheme invites customers to pay an annual fee based on 10 per cent of the contract price of the furniture being stored, but that sum may be recouped through an extra 10 per cent discount which is being offered on all items purchased by customers entering the scheme, up to the cost of the annual fee.

Of course, nobody can offer a disaster plan that will entirely cover every – or indeed any – crisis. All companies are vulnerable in their own individual way, and all disasters are unique.

Even so, there is a standard team of professionals to whom all are likely to turn – and it was this that inspired the formation in 1991 of a consortium called Total Crisis Management.

Comprising Alexander Stenhouse, Denton Hall Burgin & Warren, Ogilvy Adams & Rinehart and Touche Ross, it offers expertise in the fields of, respectively, insurance, law, public relations, and accountancy and management.

As George Weldon, a partner in Touche Ross Management Consultants, explains, the consortium aims to help clients to anticipate problems and to have an action plan of who does what, where and how, that can be immediately adopted in the event of catastrophe.

It also provides practical advice about making insurance claims, the legal situation, handling the media and establishing clear lines of communication. Just as important, it ensures that companies have allotted management responsibility in advance, so that in the immediate aftermath some managers are exclusively assigned to handle the disaster, while others are free to keep the business going.

'If you are prepared, when something does happen you are ready to leap into action,' George Weldon says, adding that this is vital to reassure not just employees and customers, but also shareholders. 'You have to respond positively, and quickly, because if you do not, the business will swiftly run down and losses will build up.'

It is important to remember that, although there will be an initial surge of goodwill towards a company that has suffered a disaster, this will soon evaporate if that firm appears to be floundering, or is making a complete mess of things.

Yet for all the planning, how do you know that your strategies will work? Well, you can now have a realistic practice run thanks to a software system designed by St Albans-based Psychometric Research & Development.

Called CriSys, the system simulates crises and disasters as an aid to training, and for exercising and refining crisis and emergency plans. And it is capable of generating a different customised 'disaster' each time it is run, complete with news broadcasts and tricky questions from a hostile Press.

Although CriSys was originally developed in conjunction with European Vinyls corporation – and consequently focused on potential disasters connected with hazardous chemicals – it can be adapted to simulate a host of horrors. Product liability and recall, kidnap or threat to senior executives, software failure or corruption, malicious tampering with IT systems, serious fraud . . . the list is quite chilling.

So how does a company start preparing for the worst? Clearly they should start by undertaking an audit of the risks so that a plan can be drawn up to ensure that continuity of operations can be maintained.

Speaking at a recent conference, CURM's managing director Chris Powell, put it: 'One thing is certain, disasters will continue to occur, as sure as night follows day. But a major fire, explosion or other disaster can have substantially different consequences for similar organisations, depending on the success or otherwise of their advance planning and the defence systems that have been put in place.'

ANALYSIS:

Who   Total Crisis Management consortium;
When   formed 1991;
Where   address/phone number not given, but 'Circle ref 155' at the end refers to a postcard bound into the magazine. This will be sent to TCM who will contact the reader direct.
Why   in case your company is hit by a disaster;
What   offer expertise;
How   action plans and practice run of CriSys software.

SPITE AND INDISCRETION

Do beware that in an effort to make the profile different, some celebs can be spiteful or be indiscreet.

Example   'Of course, I tend to get better parts than Desmond. But then, what can you expect? I mean he looks constantly tired out – it must be from all those little boys he dallies with.' Yes, it's juicy, but you'd be straight into a suit for libel if you put that in your write-up.

Example 'Between training sessions a colleague of mine took odd jobs. One was in a confectionery factory. Most of the workforce were Greek. One of the women told him how they were grateful to the British who liberated them from the Germans during World War II, and let them come to Britain to work and live, as their own villages had been flattened by the occupying troops.

As the story unfolded she told him of one Greek factory worker. He had collaborated with the Germans during the occupation. When he'd been working at the factory for two months he suddenly disappeared and hasn't been seen since.'

A tremendous story – a kangaroo court death sentence. But by mentioning it in the write-up the journalist is opening a whole can of worms.

The factory is still in operation today and even if the employees are now retired, they will still be traceable through their pension payments. DON'T DO IT. Always think of the possible repercussions of anything you write.

INTRIGUING QUOTES

How often have you read a news feature or profile and been impressed by the tremendous quotes? You wonder how journalists discover these extremely articulate and well informed people.

The answer is that probably only some of them were original thoughts from the interviewee. The rest were interesting nuggets of information that the journalist discovered through research.

At the interview he drops the fact into the ear of his subject and asks their opinion:

Q I read/heard the other day that President X has had no less than four mistresses during his term of office. Would you say this has in any way affected his job?

A Four? Really. Well, bully for him, but this could be the reason he made such a hash of the Peninsular War.

In your write-up you put: 'John Smith blames President X's blunder over the Peninsular War on the fact that he's had no less than four mistresses during his term of office.'

UNCONSCIOUS RIDICULE

When writing the profile, don't drop your interviewee in the mire by using EVERYTHING she said if she's unconsciously ridiculed herself.

Example

'How did you get the idea for your latest book?'

'Well I was having lunch with two of the Beatles, the Archbishop of Canterbury and the Prime Minister and I thought . . .'

It continues:

'How do you create such authentic dialogue for your characters?'

'Funny you should ask – only last week the Princess Royal asked me the same question . . .'

And so on – yes, she may be telling the truth, but his blatant name-dropping in print would make your interviewee look a right twit social climber.

Other bloomers I've actually had said to me by interviewees that I would not use are:

'Are you doing a promotional tour?'

'Yes. I'll be doing it in my chauffeured, 1993 Roller – you must have seen it parked outside, the powder blue one.' And:

'I did a stint on a local rag some years ago. At the next desk to mine was X who has also gone on to become a household name and respected literary lion.'

Sycophancy isn't a tool of the professional journalist, only the pathetic little scribbler who hasn't the creativity or integrity to do better.

MARKETING TIPS

And don't forget the help you get when reading your own trade press. *Writers News* and *Writers' Monthly* give useful marketing tips in every edition.

EXERCISE

Choose three printed features from any newspapers or magazines and analyse them apropos Who, What, When, Where, Why, How.

CHAPTER 20

More on Writing it Up

- Check facts
- Check at the interview
- Emotion
- Controversy
- Fog Index
- Style
- Repetition
- Tenses
- No ego trip

- Their words
- Day in the life of
- Acknowledgement
- What is it?
- Four-letter words
- The End
- Criteria
- Exercise.

HERE ARE a few odds and sods that you need to know – plus a few tips on style.

CHECK FACTS

Before you write up anything at all that's official, scandalous, illegal etc, DOUBLE CHECK. Remember, it's not the editor's job to check facts. He holds you 100 per cent responsible for what you write – so will the judge.

Check facts with another person and figures with published sources. Too many people either lie or tell you things they believe to be true but which are actually only third-hand hearsay or perhaps a fantasy account of the way they WANTED it to be.

Even with simple things, it takes an extremely noble human being to tell you: 'I was in the wrong . . .'; 'I missed the train so I wasn't even there . . .'; 'I lost . . .'; 'I was wearing the wrong clothes . . .'; 'I'm not clever enough to understand the . . .'

And downright devious people can con you into all sorts of stories which, when made public, will result in them selling more X or being given more X.

. Don't naïvely trust everything you're told:

Example A police constable friend of mine was called to a building society that had been held up. There were four witnesses and my friend spoke to each individually.

One said the get-away vehicle was: 'some sort of dark car, probably a Ford, but I can't remember its number.' Another said: 'it was a blue, four-door saloon.' Another said: 'it was a dark-blue Volvo' and the last one swore it was 'a small, black van'.

The vehicle was later found. It was a dark blue Volvo saloon.

They were all telling the truth as they remembered it.

CHECK AT THE INTERVIEW

If you're uncertain about a point made by your interviewee, ring them back a couple of days later. Don't say: 'You said you've won 23 fights in 1994, is that right?' Instead say: 'Sorry, but my tape's a bit fuzzy in places – how many fights did you say you won in 1994?'

Let's say you suspect that your interviewee may have a rather casual approach to the truth. Inform them at the beginning of the interview how well you've researched them in preparation for today. And YOU aren't lying, you HAVE done your homework thoroughly. This will usually result in them thinking: 'Well, I'd better tell it right.'

EMOTION

And if you don't want to perpetrate gutter press tactics, you won't stoop to tricks to get 'agony shots' to accompany your write-up.

It's a sad fact that Smut and Sensationalism Sells Newspapers. Far more people read the tabloid newspapers than the broadsheets – but they've made 'journalism' into a dirty word. The more up and coming journalists who demonstrate their integrity, the more the profession can begin to hold up its head again.

These two anecdotes are true:

A famous film star became addicted to alcohol. He went into a clinic to be dried out. Cured, he left there with his wife and kids. Waiting on the steps were the Press.

Were the journalist and cameraman there for a 'happy family' story? No. Happy families are boring. They don't sell newspapers.

So as not to let the facts get in the way of a good story, the reporter took along a bottle of whisky. Just before the actor came through the clinic door the journalist put the bottle on the ground in the middle of the doorway.

As he predicted, when the actor emerged he picked up the bottle so as not to trip over it. The photographer had his finger on the button.

The picture that appeared was of the actor leaving with a bottle in his hand and his wife beside him looking disapproving. The caption ran: 'After all, he couldn't leave it alone.'

A seven-year-old girl was raped then murdered. At the police station her mother, stunned after so much questioning by the police, social workers and Press looked drained and expressionless and turned to leave.

This wouldn't do for the gutter press – they've got to have agony.

One of the journalists called out: 'Mrs Jones.' As the mother looked up he threw a doll into her arms.

As predicted the woman burst into tears. The photographer got his picture.

I don't know how the journalists and cameramen can carry the guilt of despicable ploys like these.

Or perhaps I can. I was speaking to a staffer on one of the tabloids who had just written a meticulous and thorough character assassination of a pop star. The celeb in question was bringing a £1 million libel suit. I asked the journalist how he could live with himself after writing such muck. He said: 'The money – I got a £60,000 bonus.'

My only comment can be that if such a large number of people didn't buy the tabloids, then there wouldn't be the money to give the reporters bonuses.

NB: There's no legal aid for libel cases. Tabloid editors rely on the fact that the vast majority of the people they libel could never afford to take them to court.

CONTROVERSY

I'm not in any way saying don't write copy that is controversial, shocking, ludicrous, blackly funny or incisive. Just don't do it at the expense of somebody's dignity, sensitivity or anguish.

OK, OK, I don't mean professional baddies and villains. Sometimes print is the only way of attacking them. And reporting that the current screen heart-throb fell off his horse is only going to cause him some embarrassment, not anguish. I'm talking about printing malicious attacks or revelations about the general run of celebrities and Mrs-and-Mr-Everybody.

Tina Brown, editor of *Tatler* and *Vanity Fair* and wife of legendary *Times* editor Harold Evans, had this to say in an interview in the *Weekend Guardian*:

'Newspapers are losing readership because they are bland and gutless.

'It takes much courage to risk mugging at a local dinner party or cancelled ads because of a report that really hit home.

'But magazine editors know that flak of this kind is healthy . . . Flak means you're hot. Newspapers have gotten far too quiet, far too bland . . . Every so often you have to bite the hand that reads you.'

FOG INDEX

One of my students asked me to tell her how pieces were written for the 'quality' Press and 'the others'. She just wanted it on a plate. The only way to discover this AND to be able to 'digest' the discovery so you can benefit from it, is to read both a tabloid and a broadsheet newspaper daily and compare styles.

The Fog Index (or Clarity Index) was devised to define these styles – to discover the text's comprehensibility. The LOWER the Fog Index, the LARGER number of people can understand it. As a very rough guideline the newspaper ratings are:

19 *Sun* and *Star*
21 *Mirror*
28 *Express*
30 *Mail* and *Telegraph*
43 *Independent*, *Guardian*, *Times* and *Financial Times*

Now I did these very quickly and from only one example each. A more accurate rating is to quantify three pieces of text from each paper, add up the three answers, divide by three, and there you have the mean average.

This is the formula:

1 From any piece of continuous text count 200 words;
2 Count the number of major punctuation marks (.,;:?-) within those 200 words, to give you answer 'A';
3 Divide 200 by 'A' – to give answer 'B';
4 Now add up the number of words with three or more syllables, to give you answer 'C';
5 Halve 'C' to give you answer 'D';
6 Add together 'B' and 'D' to give you the Fog Index.

As a rule of thumb, below 20 is too staccato, above 40 is too literary, perhaps too much padding and long words for the sake of long words.

Most people in conversation unconsciously use an index of about 30. If you bear the reader in mind and write as you speak, then your index will be around 30.

STYLE

Be reassured – your own style WILL develop. And it will be unique because it's born from the same womb as your unique personality.

I see nothing wrong in you, as a beginner, reading pieces written by other journalists and emulating them. You will never completely duplicate (or want to duplicate) the style of, say, Kilroy-Silk, Lynn Barber or Paul Routledge. But if you feel happy writing in their particular manner, then try it. Much learning starts with copying the masters.

REPETITION

Don't sabotage your style with repetition of:

(a) Clichés – they are someone else's invention. Using them will restrict the development of your own personal style. You don't need examples – if you've heard it before, then it's a cliché.
(b) A word used more than once within the same sentence or paragraph.

Example   Gregory is determined to be another Nureyev and become famous. He said: 'I'm determined to be the best dancer since Nureyev – I want to be famous.'

This example has two repetitions – and you can't alter the words in the quote.

Try this instead:

Gregory plans to make his name a ballet byword by becoming the most talented male dancer in London, Paris and New York – bar none. He said: 'I'm determined to be the best dancer since Nureyev – I want to be famous.'

· Buy your own copy of *Roget's Thesaurus* and keep it at your elbow.

And don't be arrogantly hung up on insisting that your style shows you learned Latin at school or have a degree in Greats. You owe it to your readers – ALL your readers – to make your copy easy to read and understand. A writing style that is clear, simple and graphic goes a long way towards 'getting the message off the page'.

TENSES

Still on style – a colleague of mine has a useful ploy. As often as possible he puts the interviewer's comments in the PRESENT TENSE. This gives the words more immediacy.

NO EGO TRIP

Some beginner journalists get so enamoured with the idea of their name in print that they spew out a stream of personal opinion, witticisms and observations. But the editor won't accept a load of self-indulgent waffle about the lovely/dreadful journey you had visiting your interviewee, and what you wore and how fraying it was for your nerves. That's so amateur and should have been left behind in your fifth-form essays.

The profile is not a vehicle for your self-glorification. A professional journalist focuses the reader's attention on the interviewee from the opening sentence.

And it's not the journalist's job to agree or disagree with them. It's the interviewee's opinions the readers pay to read. Keep your suppositions for when some editor invites you to do a 'think piece' or when you're reviewing books or plays.

THEIR WORDS

An ideal profile is where the subject tells the story almost entirely in their own words with only a modicum of linking narrative from you.

Sometimes their comments will hang them from the yardarm of credibility (if you're lucky), or make the reader say 'Cor!' or 'Ah, poor thing'. What you want is to touch the reader's emotions and make them react. That's good journalism.

DAY IN THE LIFE OF

A student once brought into class a feature packed with excitement and incident called *A Day In The Life Of A Cambridge Coach*. (Let's not have jokes about 'How often did they change the horses?', please). This was coaching rowers for THE boatrace. The student marvelled at the writer's action-packed day, and said she'd love to have a try at something similar.

I agreed that it was good copy – as long as she had a week or two to spare. This type of profile needed a really dedicated journalist.

The reader thinks they get a fly on the wall view while the undertaker/tennis coach/ambulance driver/mercenary jumps through their professional hoops for 24 hours. And the journalist must have had a terrific time running alongside with a tape recorder.

But all is not as it seems. The 'day' was more than likely an entire week – even two. And the journalist did a lot less taking-notes-on-the-run than standing around bored witless while the interviewee did the tedious bits (which weren't mentioned in the write-up because they don't make good copy).

No, it's not cheating. Good journalism is entertaining as well as informative. *A Fortnight in the Life of a Circus Clown* doesn't have the same immediacy, does it? There's nothing detrimental in compressing the time scale.

ACKNOWLEDGEMENT

Please – do remember to ACKNOWLEDGE any quotes you extract from printed or broadcast material. Something along the lines of: 'as John Journalist said in *The Independent* . . .' or '. . . said Anthea Author in her book *Creative Bullying*' or 'as Prof Erudite said in *The Lancet* . . .' or '. . . explained Charles Critic in *Kaleidoscope*.'

Apart from being a courtesy, and a copyright requirement if you take more than 30 words, the acknowledgement adds weight to your piece – makes it more authentic.

WHAT IS IT?

Should your interviewee be, or comment on, anything that could be in any way unusual or obscure, do remember to EXPLAIN what it is. Five private students of mine interviewed a music therapist I brought in, and they all wrote very creditable pieces. But they hadn't analysed their final write-ups using the WWWWWH catechism. None of them explained WHAT a music therapist was.

You can happily expect your readers to be familiar with people like a bus conductor, dentist or school teacher as they're facets of everyday life. But never over-estimate their knowledge.

FOUR-LETTER WORDS

This is where you use your judgement as to whether or not to leave them in. Your subject said it, yes, but people usually rely on you to 'clean up' the comments before they go into print.

Factors you need to take into account:

(a) Does it really add anything? A 'nothing' interview, memorable only because Bob Big Star said 'Fuck the producer', is pathetic journalism.

(b) The market will often dictate that you find a substitute. Quite a few editors know that this lack of taste will lose readers, so they wouldn't accept expletives.

On the other hand, for some magazines aimed at young, fast-lane movers, profanities are almost obligatory. Study your market.

(c) Does the word sit happily on the subject's shoulders, ie fit in with their image? Most people swear and say rude things in private that they wouldn't in public. If you've done a thorough 'putting-them-at-ease' job and they're rapping away like an old friend of yours, they tend to forget that there's a write-up after the interview that's for public consumption.

(d) Discretion on your part shouldn't be an optional extra.

THE END

Don't type 'The End' merely because you've run out of steam.
Good endings need working on. They should be positive, not
like the fizzle of a damp squib.

Read the top names who write in newspapers and magazines.
Copy their types of endings. They often sum up what they've
just written and/or talk about future plans.

Examples

Paul Routledge in *The Observer*, ending a feature on the
TUC:

'Echoing George Woodcock's existentialist question "What
are we here for?" (he never offered an answer), the power
station managers suggest a radical study "not of structures and
policies, but of the proper role for the TUC at the start of yet
another hostile five years".

'I wonder if the brothers will find time to talk about THAT?'
ENDS

Jan Moir in *The Guardian*, profiling journalist Lynn Barber:

'There can be no doubt that she still thinks she is a clever
person, but underneath all the rinkly-tinkly laughter, she's a
hard-working craftswoman who could teach many of us a thing
or two about the job.

'She crosses her sandalled feet, lights another cigarette. I
jot in my notebook: toenails could do with a bit of a trim.'
ENDS

Sally Brampton in *Marie Claire* profiling fashion designer
Jasper Conran:

'Unbeknown to Shirley (his mother), he got himself a place
at Parson's School of Design where he was to study fashion.
"When I told her, she went mad. Told me I couldn't stay. I
threw my passport out of the window. We were six floors up
in the middle of Manhattan." He stayed. She left.

' "I remember walking down Fifth Avenue and I was free. It was the most incredible moment of my life. I thought, I can do what I like, be whoever I want."

· 'Jasper Conran laughs and then suddenly opens his mouth wide and screams. It is the sound of pure pleasure.' *ENDS*

Jonathan King in the London *Evening Standard*, profiling ex-Beatle Paul McCartney:
'Personally, I've always found Paul a decent fellow. He has taste . . . But like a drug, he can't give it up. He may have dropped the mildly addictive habits of his youth, but he's hooked on the big one – being a worldwide megastar. Under the surface there's a very unhappy moptop.

'I'll bet a large part of McCartney at 50 wishes he'd never had that first hit.' *ENDS*

Lester Middlehurst in the *Daily Mail*, a profile (obituary) of Press cameraman Bernard Hesketh:
'He was in the front line of nearly every war zone since 1954 . . . He was a fearless man . . . a demon. He rationalised it all by saying that when you are looking at a battle through a camera it somehow distanced you from the danger.

'Although he was very, very brave he was also a sensitive man. When he went to film the Colombian earthquake he broke down in tears when he saw a young girl drowning.

'He wanted to film her but didn't feel he could. So he just smiled at her, she smiled back and gestured him to film. He cried like a child afterwards.' *ENDS*

Hilary Kingsley in the *Sunday Mirror Magazine*, profiling Ian McShane:
'McShane has made Lovejoy into the perfect man-you'd-most-like-to-reform, a national treasure to be preserved for British women.

'All right, he's getting on a bit – he must be halfway to an antique himself. He's home now. And the Government should think twice before issuing another export licence.

'If McShane does go back to the Yanks, I will have only one thing to say about it – MCSHAME.' *ENDS*

CRITERIA

Here is a checklist – the main points you need to verify after you've written the piece, to see if it's saleable.

You should be able to answer yes to every question:

- **Market** – is the topic and treatment right for the readership?
- **Style** – is it written in the house style, the 'voice' of the publication you want to sell it to?
- **Length** – does it have the number of words the editor specified?
- **Headline** – is it short, with a verb – not a mere label?
- **Opening** – does intro have impact and compel reader to read on?
- **Angle** – is it original, really NEW, or been done before?
- **Who, What, Where, When, Why, How** – are they all there?
- **Quotes** – are there plenty of them, to give human interest?
- **Libel** – could anything be construed as libellous?
- **Facts** – have they all been checked and re-checked?
- **Topical** – do I have the very latest facts?
- **Clichés** – is the piece free of trite phrases?
- **Repetition** – are there synonyms to replace repetitions?
- **Sentences** – are they no longer than 27 words?
- **Language** – short words, active not passive, non-verbose?
- **Syntax** – are grammar, tenses and punctuation correct?
- **Spelling** – are all doubtful words checked, especially names?
- **Argument** – is it balanced, both sides presented?
- **Focus** – have I stuck to the point and not deviated?
- **Ending** – does it round off the piece effectively, possibly mentioning future plans?
- **Presentation** – is it typed and laid out professionally (see page 234)?

EXERCISE

Work out the Fog Index of a feature or profile taken from:

1 An upmarket periodical;
2 A mid-market periodical;
3 A down-market periodical.

CHAPTER 21

Selling It

- Sell first, write second
- What is a commission?
- Write for the reader
- No unsolicited work
- Fiercely competitive
- Possible markets
- Contacting the editor
- Thirty seconds
- Write yourself a script
- Kill fees
- Pseudonyms
- First impression
- How to lay out a typescript
- Word processing and typing
- Exercise.

AGAIN, so as to be fair to readers of *Journalism for Beginners*, I'm trying not to repeat too much here – but some repetition is inevitable. If some of the points here seem to be covered only superficially, then that's because they are covered in depth in the first book.

SELL FIRST, WRITE SECOND

It's common knowledge in the trade that while amateurs talk about writing, professionals talk about marketing.

Professional journalists sell their work BEFORE they write it. OK – so you're not a professional YET – but that's what you're aiming for.

It makes sense to sound out the market to find out if what you want to write will sell, before you go to all the trouble of research/interview/write. No successful journalist would sur-

vive if s/he wasted hours/days working on something that isn't
going to be accepted by an editor.

Chapter 3 covered 'approaching the editor' before you even
started the research. And this is the best move. But if you
couldn't sell it, let's say you went ahead anyway hoping to sell
it 'on spec' once the piece was completed. This is what I'm
covering in this chapter.

WHAT IS A COMMISSION?

It's rare for beginners to be given commissions because the
editor hasn't seen what they can do. The editor needs to know
he can rely on the piece being in the right style, to the right
length, non-verbose, facts checked, delivered on deadline and
many, many other facets that make the piece 'professional'.
The way he does that is by reading cuttings you send him of
work you've written that's already IN PRINT.

Let me define 'commission'. You make the initial approach
to an editor by phone or in writing. During that conversation/
correspondence the editor makes a firm promise to use and
pay for your piece BEFORE even seeing it. That's known as
'commissioning the work'. Immediately after they've said that
you ALWAYS ask: 'Are you giving me a commission?' If the
answer is 'Yes', then a verbal contract exists in law. As soon
as you put down the phone you WRITE AND CONFIRM it,
repeating what the editor agreed to.

If all the editor has said is: 'I'm interested, I'll consider it'
or 'Yes, I'll look at it', that isn't enough, it isn't a commission.
And that's what they say 99 per cent of the time.

As a beginner, you won't have any cuttings of your work in
print to send to the publication. The best you can hope for
from an editor is a verbal pledge that she or he WILL read it.
And that, by the way, is what you say to your potential interviewee when you make the vital initial phone call to arrange
to meet them.

You say: 'The editor of X SAYS S/HE IS INTERESTED.'
Those are the words you use. I doubt very much if the potential
interviewee would then ask you: 'Does this mean you have a

commission?' as the general public are not aware of the difference. By saying: 'the editor has said s/he's interested', that SOUNDS as though you have a commission. It's then up to you to turn out a really professional piece of work so the editor will actually buy it.

WRITE FOR THE READER

Journalist and author of *How to Write and Sell Travel Articles* Cathy Smith says: 'One of the hardest lessons a freelance writer must learn is to direct work to a specific audience.'

If you want editors to publish your work you can't subjectively write what YOU want. You must OBJECTIVELY define what the READER WANTS.

The sooner you understand that journalists are in the retail trade, the sooner you'll start selling your work.

Example Let's say you're passionate about white, full-length crinoline dresses if you're female – scarlet tabards and tights if you're male. You look great in them, you really DO look good. They show off your curves/muscles and give you confidence.

As you can guess, if you stock your entire shop with these items your business would soon be in the hands of the receivers. It's SUBJECTIVE stock-keeping.

To make a success of your clothes shop you need to study trends – what's being worn now? what are the majority of people buying? In other words, what do customers WANT?

Yes, of course, everyone knows this.

So why do most beginner writers produce work totally unsuitable for today's market?

Because they haven't studied the trends. They haven't spent a couple of hours in the public library and the largest newsagents they can find studying and analysing the magazines and newspapers to see what readers are buying. Therefore, they don't know each publication's 'Reader Profile', their target readership.

Many of them WON'T do it because they arrogantly put themselves on a pedestal and come out with that old chestnut: 'I won't prostitute my art.'

That sort of thinking is purely amateur and a whole load of manure. Well, it is if they want to sell to editors of COMMER-CIAL publications – the ones sold in newsagents. (Being published in small 'private' magazines IS NOT JOURNALISM.)

If you don't go into libraries/newsagents to STUDY magazines and newspapers (known as MARKET RESEARCH), then you're doomed to be an unpublished amateur.

To the editor, specific angling means the difference between a yes and a yawn.

NO UNSOLICITED WORK

And searching for a magazine to offer my piece to, what would be the first thing I'd check? Whether they ACCEPT unsolicited (i.e. non-commissioned) contributions from journalists. If they DON'T accept unasked-for pieces written on spec there will be a statement somewhere in the publication saying so – it will say something along the lines of 'unsolicited work not considered'.

The statement will be tucked away in a corner on the contents or back page usually, and will be in minuscule letters – so you need to search.

Incidentally, there's often a statement: 'we accept no responsibility for unsolicited MS'. That means exactly what it says – written work possibly may not be returned because it got lost or binned. But look upon the statement as good news, because what it IS saying is that unsolicited work is received by that publication, they haven't banned it.

And while you're checking, if you discover that the publication you've chosen DOESN'T take unsolicited MS, then look at other magazines displayed near it on the newsagent's shelf. Similar types of magazines are usually grouped together.

FIERCELY COMPETITIVE

Always aim high. Never lose sight of your ultimate objective – the quality publications. In the case of journalism these are the national newspapers and the consumer glossy monthly magazines.

But let's be realistic.

Journalism has CHANGED RADICALLY in the last few years. Not the demand – this still remains 'high quality writing with an original angle'. No, what has altered is the competition.

The recession has meant many staffers being made redundant. What do they do? They go freelance.

So the freelance pool for editors to fish in has been gradually stocked with bigger fish, i.e. journalists who know exactly what editors want AND have a good track record of printed work. Many are also editors' pals.

The bad news for you is that today, top publication editors will seldom even look at work from an unknown.

So for you that means be realistic about the very top publications. Perhaps for, say, a year, until you've made a name for yourself, focus on local and regional newspapers, specialist magazines, the trade press, the more down-market women's press and the freebie newspapers and newsmagazines.

Concentrate on building up a portfolio of PRINTED work (you can't send editors copies of work you've written but not had published). The criterion is very simple – published work is success, unpublished is failure. Editors aren't interested in failures.

Look upon this period as your apprenticeship when you're learning the trade and building up contacts. THEN you've a fair chance of competing with those ready-made, ex-staff, professional freelances out there.

POSSIBLE MARKETS

Some of the best consumer publications to try for profiles and features are newsmagazines. These are more likely to accept contributions by beginner journalists. Among the freebies are the job vacancy newsmags given out at tube/train stations and bus termini such as (in London) *Ms London*, *Girl About Town* and *Midweek*. Many big cities have their equivalents. And nationally there are the newsmags you pay for such as *Best*, *Bella*, *Take-a-Break* and *Chat*.

They all like profiles of celebs and of people who do something unusual or achieve something worthwhile. The last four particularly like TOTs – Triumph Over Tragedy stories. These are mini-profiles on people who have overcome any type of heavy trauma – serious illness, emotional experience, been the victim of an attack.

If you're into writing up social issues the women's magazines are your biggest market, including the women's pages of the newspapers. The freebie job vacancy newsmagazines given out at tube stations also like social issues.

Looking at recent copies of the freebies (below), the topics could have easily been handled by beginner journalists:

- Cardboard City – *interviews* with London's homeless;
- Hostages of Fortune – *interviews* with businessmen taking classes to learn how to cope with being kidnapped;
- Violence on the Streets – *interviews* with women who don't go out at night because they've been mugged or know women who have been.

Another publication, a newsmag, that specialises in profiles is *Hello!* Now they also take a few TOTs, but their *raison d'être* is picture profiles of the rich and famous. The vast majority of the profiles are bought in from picture agencies and most of the rest of the people interviewed are tracked down by Contessa Varella. She has a vast network of international high society contacts and is paid a retainer by *Hello!*

But if you know someone that she doesn't, AND you're also a crack photographer, then the editor would be interested to hear from you. Don't underrate the pictures – this is photo-journalism and the words are subservient to the images.

Readers want the rich and famous 'doing their thing'. They want to know about their houses, lifestyle, clothes and all the accoutrements and events the monied enjoy, such as polo matches and hunt balls.

Hello! is fantasy reading for the plebs. It's one of the most successful publications on the market, selling half a million copies every week.

Be aware that the *Hello!* journalist NEVER 'puts down' the royalty, presidents, aristocracy, socialites, *nouveaux riches*, stars of screen, stage and sport that they interview.

And similar in content is *OK*, launched April 1993. Their reader profile is 'mainly female between ages 18 to 45', an important point to remember when you're interviewing for that magazine. The editor says 'most of the profiles are bought from freelances.' They prefer a WRITTEN outline with examples of work in print.

By the way, *OK* are interested only in British celebrities.

If you're stuck for a publication to write for look in the *Writers' & Artists' Yearbook* and *The Writer's Handbook*. They're published annually in the autumn and give details of the editorial needs of publications on British and overseas markets. But being yearbooks, the information you want could be months out of date as, because of the recession, some publications change their policies overnight.

CONTACTING THE EDITOR

OK, so you've found a couple of publications that you hope might be interested in your write-up. So now to contact the features editor or editor. There are two methods – in writing or by phone.

1 *WRITTEN CONTACT*   Most editors prefer you to write – but they do take ages to reply. I give an example of an outline letter in Chapter 3.
2 *PHONE CONTACT*   As editors take ages to reply, if you have an idea for a TOPICAL news feature, you can't wait for six months for an answer or the war might be over or the inventor of the widget gone abroad. So you ring them.

Now, there are good times to ring daily newspaper editors and bad times. Never at 3.30PM or for a couple of hours after because that slot is scheduled for the editorial meeting for the following day's edition.

You ALWAYS ask for the features editor or editor by NAME – very important, this. How do you find out what her name is? Look on the masthead of the publication – or ask the switchboard operator.

THIRTY SECONDS

Because every editor and features editor is furiously busy, when you're put through you've got thirty seconds to interest her/him in what you have to sell or s/he could hang up on you. You go straight to the point, no preamble – 'Hello, my name is X, I'm a journalist and I have an idea you might be interested in' – none of that. You describe first the theme and then the angle – all in your initial sentence.

Example 'Would you be interested in 1,500 words on cohabitation contracts – the angle is "should they be a prelude to marriage or an alternative?" The latest figures show there are 1.2 million people cohabiting in the UK.

'I've interviewed ten couples, some with cohabitation contracts, some without, some married. All have relevant and emotive comments. One homeless woman could have had her partner's flat if there'd been a contract. A man who admits society was set up by men on their terms, so a woman live-in lover *needs* a contract. A couple whose child had to leave private school when they broke up because the man was the breadwinner – she's now deep into a court case. A gay couple who have a contract.

'I've also interviewed a Relate counsellor, a psychologist and a solicitor.'

That's my pitch and it took less than thirty seconds for the 'angle' and less than a minute for the rest of the outline.

WRITE YOURSELF A SCRIPT

Points like this have to be well thought out BEFORE you phone. What you do to ensure you verbalise the idea clearly and concisely is to type something along the lines of the above and read it to the editor.

Paste it at the top of an A4 size blank page well over on the left to leave lots of space for you to note the editor's answers. And list down the left-hand side other questions you need answers to assuming s/he says 'yes', e.g. Do you need photos?

Writing a script applies also and particularly to the initial phone call when you try and sell the idea before you write it (see Chapter 3). Questions you could add then are:

- Are there any other points you would like included?
- When do you want this by?
- Is this a commission?

Using a written script gives you three advantages:

1 It ensures you ask all the questions you want to. When you're actually on the phone you'll naturally be a trifle nervous, and even well-thought-out questions will simply go out of your head.
2 It saves the editor's time, if you get straight to the point without hesitating and bumbling. It gives him the impression of a professional, and therefore gives him confidence in you.
3 You have a record of what YOU said and what HE said. This is vital because as soon as you put down the phone, you type a letter of confirmation. You repeat all that was said. This is invaluable should there be some dispute about the feature in the future – the editor could leave and his successor might say she doesn't want your piece; if a fee has been discussed this will be the only written record of how much, the editor might have forgotten to note it down, or might lose it anyway. A confirmation letter is a real ally.

With a profile the approach is just the same – give the editor the ANGLE in the first 30 seconds. Don't just say: 'Would you be interested in a profile on Jeffrey Archer?' and wait for them to say: 'Not another one on him (yawn) – no thanks.' You must explain the ANGLE straight away – 'he has a new book', or 'his book is being made into a film' – whatever.

KILL FEES

Should you get a pledge from a magazine that they're interested, do the interview, send the editor the profile or news feature, and eighteen months later it's not in print – what do you do? This does occasionally happen – for various editorial reasons, not because your piece isn't good enough.

Perhaps the celebrity's publicist contacts you: 'I thought you said *The Guardian* promised to publish it?' You then contact the editor – explain the problem. You'll get any one of a number of replies from: 'We never received it' or 'We lost it' to 'Sorry, brilliant piece, we had it slotted for the 6th January edition, but something more topical came up and we had to shelve it. We've taken it down and dusted it off a few times, but now I'm afraid it's far too old. Sorry and all that.'

What you say is: 'OK – I'll accept a kill fee.' You don't ask for it back because they know all professionals keep a copy.

Kill Fee is jargon – it's a payment in lieu of being published. It's an acknowledgement by the editor that although he doesn't intend to print your piece, it's written professionally and he was enthusiastic enough to agree to you writing it for him in the first place, and to tell you he'd use it. In view of all the work you had to do, he offers a fee because he 'killed' the piece, i.e. didn't print it. This is not an unusual occurrence, especially with national newspapers.

Don't abandon the piece. You then find out the publication date of the novelist's next book, or the star's next film or concert, or the sportsman's next match (whoever you interviewed). When you know, peddle the idea around other publications. When you've got a bite, ring the publicist and ask him to arrange for you to ring the Big Name for a brief call, for you to UP-DATE the piece, get a few recent quotes – and you're back in business. In other words, don't ever give up on a good idea.

PSEUDONYMS

A student of mine, Mark, asked me: 'If an editor turns you down, can you try again using a pen name?'

Not really. If he didn't like it the first time he's not going to change his mind – especially as he could be receiving contributions from dozens of journalists every day and is not short of material.

But suppose you're convinced that the theme is a good one, then what you could do is come up with an ENTIRELY DIFFERENT ANGLE.

If you asked for the editor the first time, on your second phone call ask for the features editor.

A thought to type out and stick on your wall above your work processor – REJECTION HURTS, BUT IT DOESN'T DAMAGE ME IRREVOCABLY.

First Impression

As John Diamond, writing in the *Guardian* says: 'Given the average editor's tendency to bin anything that's obviously the work of an amateur, it's as well to look as if you know what you're doing.'

First impressions are very powerful. The first thing the editor sees when s/he picks up your piece – even before they get into reading it – is the PRESENTATION.

The LAYOUT of the piece is extremely important. If you don't follow all the following points, then the editor could jettison your piece as he takes it from the envelope:

Professionals Lay Out Typescripts as Follows:

1 NB: Handwritten work will not be read.
2 Always type on ONE SIDE of WHITE, A4 size, 80 gsm paper.
3 *Top of Page 1 [right hand side]* Author's name, address and telephone number, also fax number if you have one.
4 *Top of Page 1 [left hand side]* Number of words, under that, serial rights offered, e.g. FBSR, 2nd BSR, N.Am.FSR etc.
5 *Under that, and CENTRE* Headline, and under that your by-line, using a pseudonym if you want to.
6 Set MARGINS at least 1½ inches/4 cms wide ALL ROUND [this space is for the editor to make printer's marks].

7 NEVER justify right-hand edge of type, ALWAYS justify left.

8 Start flush, but indent all paragraphs (this is not an office letter).

9 Type in DOUBLE line spacing.

10 *Top right* – number all pages.

11 *Bottom right* – always type MORE . . .

12 At the end type 'ENDS'.

And here are seven additional turn-offs for an editor which immediately brands the piece as 'amateur' and could make sure it's thrown away unread:

(a) To save paper an amateur might set the type at less than 10 or 12 characters to the inch. Don't do it.

(b) The ribbon is used till it's so faint it's barely legible. This will save money on ribbons but will infuriate the editor. Reserve your older/faintest ribbons for drafts and for the hard copy you retain on file.

(c) Any colour ribbon other than BLACK.

(d) Smudgy type because the typebars haven't been cleaned.

(e) Cheap dot matrix printout that is so 'dotty' the words are unclear.

(f) Unusual or fussy typefaces such as 'Script'.

(g) Paper is flimsy, shiny, coloured, grubby or is in an unseparated continuous sheet. Always ask your stationer for 80gsm white A4.

And I must tell you about one of my young students. She stayed behind at class to tell me, gleefully, that she'd just sent off her first written piece because an editor had said she was interested. She added proudly, 'I studied lots of editions of the magazine like you said, and I got the editor's name and spelt it right.

'I also noticed the text in the magazine was all set in narrow columns in single-line spacing. So I didn't type the words right across the page, but in two column, also in single-line spacing so they could see I knew how they laid out their pages.'

I gently explained to her that the way the text appears on the printed page is not the concern of the writer. It's decided by the typesetter on the publication.

And it doesn't matter WHAT you submit to an editor, be it a news story, news feature, profile, review or filler – they ALL have to be typed right across the page (leaving 1½ inch margins both sides), and in double-line spacing.

WORD PROCESSING/TYPING

As editors won't read handwritten work, it's imperative to get yourself:

- a TYPEWRITER if you need to learn keyboard skills. This is only because it's cheaper than a word processor; a manual typewriter will do – or
- a WORD PROCESSOR

(a) which is ten times faster than a typewriter when editing,
(b) and because the day is approaching when editors will accept text only on disc.

Word processors and typewriters have identical 'qwerty' keyboards (qwerty refers to the layout of the keys with the alphabet and numerals on them, not the 'function' keys).

Courses in word processing and typing are available at Adult Education Centres.

Second-hand WPs and typewriters could be risky, but see adverts for them in local press, *Loot*, *Exchange & Mart*.

EXERCISE

Analyse styles

1   On the same day buy two newspapers – one must be a broadsheet, the other a tabloid (but not the *Mail* or *Express*). And they must have a news story about the same event.
2   Sit down and read them both two or three times.
3   List the differences in style such as length of words, length of sentences and use of 'sensational' and 'unsensational' words and phrases.

CHAPTER 22

Guest Speaker Darryl McElroy

- How do you start?
- Presspack
- Angles
- Move fast
- Verify doubtful facts
- Exclusives
- Rejection
- Risks

- Act professionally
- I'm nervous
- Listening
- Transcribing
- Editing
- She said, he said
- Don't show it to them.

HERE ARE SOME of the problems aired by journalism students. This is the transcript of a question and answer session at one of my classes. The course is *Interviewing for Journalists*, and our guest speaker is freelance journalist Darryl McElroy.

HOW DO YOU START?

JOAN   How does a beginner start? Is market research their first step?

DARRYL   Yes, no professional would get far without the initial market research – it's ALWAYS the first thing you have to do.

JOAN   May I start by asking you about the Greg Hoffman piece you did for a national newspaper last month? How did you get the idea in the first place?

Darryl   I was approached by his publicist. Of course it was
    different when I was a beginner, I had to start by asking
    for interviews. A student of Joan's recently got an inter-
    view with comedian Roy Hudd, just by asking his agent.
    But when you've been in journalism as long as I have,
    you'll find people come to you.

    These days journalists increasingly get stories and ideas
    from publicists. Three rang me today, two of which I can't
    use, one of which I can. In the case of Greg Hoffman, I
    had a call from this West End publicity company whom I
    have dealt with in the past.

    I knew Hoffman had just written and illustrated his
    autobiography, and I knew a little bit about him; that
    he was permanently in a wheelchair as he has no legs,
    but despite this he was essentially an achiever. I said I
    was interested.

    Then we immediately moved on to stage two which was
    them biking to me a proof copy of the autobiography, plus
    a Presspack. The minute I saw it I knew this guy was a gift
    to a journalist because he has a story that's very rich,
    human, emotional, vivid, full of achievement, and
    action-packed.

PRESSPACK

Student Jack   What's a Presspack?
Darryl   A pile of stuff from the publicist – a biography,
    bibliography, list of things he's done – a sort of CV.

    I could see a number of different angles. As soon as
    I'd read the pack I began to ring round. First there was
    a 'general' application which would interest a national
    newspaper. Here comes your market research. I thought
    this particular daily was right because they have a reputa-
    tion for running pieces – good pieces – on disabled
    people. So I rang them first and they took 800 words
    right away.

    Then, I looked at the form in which he chose to express
    himself as a photographer and writer. So I contacted a

magazine that specialises in art photography, and sold them a 3,500-word version.

Then I thought, 'the guy's a writer who's overcome many obstacles', so I rang a writers' specialist magazine and sold them a 2,000-word version.

Then I thought, this guy is disabled, so I rang a publication that is devoted to the needs of handicapped people, and sold them a 1,000-word version.

Not a word has been written yet, but I've sold four versions of this story – all DIFFERENT, in different house styles, with different slants, for different markets.

At least some of the information about Greg Hoffman will be repeated in all the versions – the basic, background stuff. But that constitutes no more than 20 per cent of each feature and it's written in a variety of ways. It's the main angle, the main theme that will be different in each case.

ANGLES

STUDENT SARAH   How exactly are the angles different?

DARRYL   In the first I'll concentrate on the man's personality, in the next on his new book, in the next on the methods he uses to actually write, and in the last on his triumph over his disability. All different aspects of the same person.

I suppose I could consider selling a version to a Javanese magazine. He lived in Jakarta for some years – I'd angle it on his childhood in a Javanese school and his keen interest in collecting live snakes – which incidentally feature quite often in his photography. And there'll be a woman's magazine, many are interested in TOTs (Triumph Over Tragedy stories). There's a vast choice of angles because he's such a complex person.

What selects the angle is what the journalist chooses to focus on, and all other elements fall back. Another thing to remember is that each readership will also be different.

JOAN   Angles are a little like cakes. The basic ingredients of
all cakes are flour, eggs and butter, say – equate that with
'background information'.

But if you then add cherries and a cream filling you've
got a Black Forest gâteau, or if you add masses of dried
fruit and icing you've got a birthday cake. They're both
cakes – but entirely different versions – it's merely that the
main accent, the main theme is different. You expand on
the angle you've chosen.

STUDENT VANESSA   Are you sure before you ring them that
all these publications will buy the angle you offer?

DARRYL   No, but apart from the magazine devoted to disabled people, for all the others I've come through with
ideas before which they've published. In that case the
editor tends to listen two minutes longer than if they
don't know you. They're going to listen right to the end
of your sentence. Your name also carries weight because
they know you can deliver the goods. Because they've
used you before, they know that you can do it the way
they want it.

And editors have a 'nose for a story'. You're 30 seconds
into explaining about Greg Hoffman and they know you've
got something.

The next stage was to arrange an interview with Hoffman – which I did through the publicist, who gave him my
phone number and me his number. Unfortunately we live
miles apart – he's in Exeter, I'm in London. But his wife's
family live in London, and we arranged for me to spend
an afternoon with him there when he was visiting them.

Knowing that I'd pre-sold at least four versions of his
story I told Greg: 'I need two hours of your time.' With a
story with so many ramifications, and so many markets
interested, I knew I'd need at least a couple of hours to
get that amount of information.

Having done that, I rang back the daily to arrange for
a photographer to be there at the same time. Most national
newspaper photographers are freelances too, so they drew
one from their pool. So I now have a date, and a time –
that's the interview set up.

That's not untypical of how most celebrity interviews happen these days. OK, he's not a BIG celebrity at the moment, but he might be one day because he has a great deal of talent. His book for instance, isn't the usual type of autobiography – it's definitely New Wave photography. I couldn't cram all that he's done in the 800 words for the newspaper – he's directed three plays, two of which he wrote, also started a club and support group for disabled people in his area – and it's flourishing – he's quite phenomenal.

MOVE FAST

STUDENT NEIL How long did it take from when you received the Presspack to when you sold the profiles?

DARRYL I was called in the morning, the Presspack arrived lunchtime, and I'd sold three of them by four o'clock. You've got to move fast. The newspaper, like all nationals, wanted it yesterday. I sold it to them on the Wednesday, did the interview on the Friday and had it on the editor's desk the following Monday.

Then they wanted a re-write – which quite often happens. They rang and said: 'We loved it' – and I knew. Always be suspicious when they say: 'We loved it,' because the next word is always 'BUT'. They wanted more clarification. The features editor had doubts about the truth of some of it. She didn't believe that a person as disabled as Greg could achieve the amount he has.

When a child, a car he was in got stuck on a level crossing – it was hit by a train and amputated both his legs. They weren't cut off low down, he was also nearly emasculated. From the age of eight he lived in hospitals having operation after operation. He has a great affection for Stoke Mandeville hospital which specialises in cases like his.

Fortunately for him, in his teens he met a professional photographer who recognised Greg's creativity and encouraged him. He proved to Greg that being legless didn't have to be a deterrent to using a camera. The photos in his book are very creative in a weird, ethereal way – totally unlike any others I've seen.

VERIFY DOUBTFUL FACTS

STUDENT NEIL   Did you have to verify the fact that he'd actually taken the photos?

DARRYL   Yes, I rang people who knew him, including the photographer who taught him. I also got the publicist's word for it, the publisher's word and *his* word too. Most of all I had my own instinct. Over the years I've interviewed hundreds of people and I think I can always tell when someone is lying – which people do now and again. Yes, Greg's photography is incredible, it would be for a fit person. Remember, he had tuition from a gifted and caring professional photographer who spent a lot of time with him because he was in the same hospital. He had spinal injuries after falling off a roof when he was filming.

EXCLUSIVES

STUDENT EMMA   Was the daily newspaper the only national you sold it to?

DARRYL   Yes – increasingly these days, national newspapers want exclusives. Not in the way that you understand a news story exclusive, but an exclusive feature. The features editor said: 'We'll have this, but we want an exclusive up to publication date.' They wanted an undertaking that no daily national would run a piece on Greg before his book appeared.

STUDENT MICHAEL   How on earth did you guarantee that?

DARRYL   I got the publisher and the publicist to write to the newspaper that same day, and get the letters round by motorbike, saying 'We guarantee not to let any other journalist have an interview before publication date.'

REJECTION

STUDENT NOEL   Have you ever been rejected?

DARRYL   Of course. Rejection is part of the process – one of the aspects of writing you have to take on board. I've met internationally acclaimed writers who regularly get rejected.

NOEL   How does that affect you?

DARRYL   It used to really affect me – now it casts me down for 15 to 20 minutes – and then I get angry. So I pick up the phone and ring somebody else. But I'll look at the piece and try and analyse what's wrong – it's usually that it's the wrong market, I haven't researched well enough. So I retype it for a different market and it goes straight out again.

RISKS

STUDENT NOEL   A mate of mine works on a local paper. He told me he'd written a sort of exposé – as a result the person he wrote about, Frank Somebody, was sued and had to pay a hefty fine. After the court case this Frank went round to my mate's newspaper office and threatened to duff him up if he didn't keep his nose out of his affairs. What can my mate do?

DARRYL   Nothing. If you're reporting 'dirty dealings' you're upholding one of the finer tenets of journalism in that you're doing a public service. BUT – yes – I don't have an answer.

This is one of the hazards of journalism – it does have its risks. But here's strength to his pen – don't let the bastards grind him down – or anyone else who wants to be a reporter.

STUDENT EMMA   For a beginner, is it a good idea to go out and buy dozens of different magazines before you start to write?

DARRYL   Not really. Market research should be selective. You've got to practise writing in the style of, say, the

Guardian, *Fear Magazine*, *Disability Now* and *Women's Own* – they're all extremely different. But, aim high; a good professional can write in the style of any publication that wants them.

ACT PROFESSIONALLY

STUDENT SALLY   When YOU approach an editor it's easy, but what about beginners, what do they do?

DARRYL   Exactly what I do. Ring them up, give as professional and confident a presentation as you can (whether or not you feel it). Offer the idea concisely, because you will have written yourself a little script before you rang – or perhaps you're writing an outline – and you're in with as much chance as the rest of us. YOU'RE ONLY AS GOOD AS YOUR PRESENTATION.

SALLY   But how do you start?

DARRYL   You say, 'Hello, my name is Sally Bloggs, I'm a freelance journalist, would you be interested in an interview with the world's tallest man.' Don't pause and give them time to think – go ahead confidently and they'll believe you're an established professional.

SALLY   But I've never had anything published, so what happens when they ask me for cuttings?

DARRYL   You give them such a brilliant idea that it grabs them, then your credentials become secondary. They may only ask you for cuttings if they're not quite taken with the idea – otherwise they're so enthusiastic, they might even forget to ask you. It happens. Get them carried away with your enthusiasm with what YOU'RE CONVINCED is a good, saleable idea. This is a Catch 22 situation – if you haven't enough initiative to find a way around it, then you'll never make a journalist anyway.

STUDENT NOEL   How long do you have to wait for their decision?

DARRYL   They'll tell you there and then on the phone whether they're genuinely interested or not. There's no such thing as a coy editor – they either want it or they don't.

STUDENT ROBERT   Could they forget?

DARRYL   You don't let them – anyway, you confirm it. On the phone you settle the number of words, deadline, rate of pay. Put down the phone, go straight to your word processor and knock out a letter . . . 'With reference to our telephone conversation today, this is to confirm that I will deliver XXX number of words on XXX (subject), by 24th February, for a fee of £XXX. Yours faithfully'. If they say in actual words 'this is a commission', and only then, you should include 'thanks for the commission'. And keep a copy.

I'M NERVOUS

STUDENT NEIL   Doesn't your nervousness as a beginner make your subject nervous?

DARRYL   In a way this is an argument *against* being nervous. Half the battle is won before they even meet you because they have a mental picture of a professional journalist who's going to ask questions.

They're not expecting someone to come and say: 'Er, um, splutter. I wonder if you . . . I mean, do you think . . . Sorry, I made a mess of that question, this isn't working, Oh woe is me, I want me Mum.' It's IMPERATIVE to convey a sense of confidence. How you actually feel is irrelevant. They can't see into your head. Their expectancy is a professional journalist, therefore, when you walk in – you're a professional journalist.

It's all role playing – we all do it every day. You're the journalist, they're the celebrity – certain well-defined actions are expected from each role-player, and those are the noises you both make.

JOAN   Look at it this way – we're all playing roles right now. You're playing the role of being students, I'm in the role of the tutor, Darryl's in the role of the guest speaker. We all know what we expect of each other – and PSYCHOLO-

GICALLY THAT MENTALLY PROGRAMMES OUR
ACCEPTANCE OF THE OTHER PERSON.

If you're not feeling too confident as a journalist, don't
let it throw you. You're lacking confidence, BUT YOUR
SUBJECT DOESN'T KNOW THAT. What he sees is a real
live journalist. The name of the game is bluff. And the
adrenalin takes over and gets you through.

LISTENING

STUDENT VANESSA   I have difficulty in LISTENING to the
interviewee – how do you take in what they're saying?

DARRYL   You interact. For me, listening is all about making
your subject feel relaxed, interacting with them, i.e. telling
them a little bit about yourself, empathising, then make
the interview a conversation.

TRANSCRIBING

STUDENT VANESSA   Tell us about transcribing – do you type
back every single word that was said?

DARRYL   No, it's a refining process – I don't put in all the
'ums', 'ers', 'you knows' and 'actuallys' – or the repetitions. A major part of the work isn't the interview, it's the
EDITING – it's what YOU make of it – that's the creative
part. It's your interpretation of what you've recorded. You
go through a number of times tightening, cutting,
smoothing, while retaining your subject's 'voice'.

But be very careful you're not so ruthless that you lose
their 'individual voice'. Everyone has their own vocabu-
lary – we don't all use the same words. When you concentrate on what makes a person individual it's also their sentence structures – they way they put words together.

For instance, the way in which they put the cart before
the horse, and some people make quite blatant grammat-
ical errors, but I'll often leave them in to retain that per-

son's 'particular flavour'. Never, of course, allow your subject to sound stupid or obscene. But, if you took out all the idiosyncrasies, every one of your subjects will sound like you. The ideal is that the reader can differentiate between you and the subject speaking.

This is one of the real problems of the writing life. The actual interviewing is a small percentage of it – most of your time is spent sitting in front of your screen and making your forehead bleed.

EDITING

STUDENT EMMA   What guidelines can you give us on writing up the actual interview – the ratio of quotes – would you transcribe it all first?

DARRYL   My life has been enormously simplified since I bought a word processor. Of all forms of journalism, the interview, once transcribed, benefits most from a WP.

I transcribe the whole of the tape on to it. But even while doing the initial process I'm weeding it – an automatic process, I'm taking out 'ers', sentences that start then peter out, repetitions.

I'm still going to be left with a great wodge of words – perhaps 10,000 to 15,000. You'll gradually develop an instinct to know what NOT to put into the machine . . . you'll censor from ear, to brain, to hand without thinking about it after you've done it a few times. THERE IS NO SUBSTITUTE FOR EXPERIENCE, FOR DOING IT – it's the only way to learn.

It's not unknown for me to revise seven, eight, nine, ten times, especially if the concepts being conveyed are particularly complicated. Perhaps the person expresses themselves in a very convoluted way. It's funny how many people, even those in the communications field, who cannot communicate verbally.

STUDENT PAUL   So you REARRANGE THEIR WORDS?

DARRYL   Yes. Some people just coming into journalism can't understand this, and they think it's a bit unethical. What you do is retain the ESSENCE of what's said without necessarily using the exact words they do.

Every professional journalist does this. Let's say someone wants to make a point, 'I wrote this book because I want to help the plight of battered wives', yet they spend 800 words telling you that. It's justifiable, indeed, beholden upon you, to put it into shape. It's part of being a wordsmith – it's your job. See yourself as a midwife, you must get out of the interviewee what it is they're actually trying to say.

But don't make up things – it's not justifiable to put quotes into their mouth. And never 'translate' words to their detriment, always to their advantage. It's standard journalistic practice to paraphrase – just as long as you're not misrepresenting them.

SHE SAID, HE SAID

STUDENT MICHAEL   How do you avoid keep saying in the write-up 'I asked her this'?

DARRYL   That's similar to fiction's 'he said' 'she said'.

There are two basic types of interview, the feature and the Q&A. I prefer the feature type, that's an article with lots of quotes, it's much more satisfying to write. It flows better, reads better and is also a more adult way of doing things. The Q&A is a sort of paperback version – I prefer hardbacks.

Some magazines will take only Q&A – *Penthouse*, for instance. The feature format gives writers much more leeway to express themselves.

Which kind of answers your original question about avoiding 'I said' – I wouldn't want to see 'I said' in any interview I wrote.

However, you need to avoid 'thesaurusitis' – he claimed, he intoned, he remarked, he vouched – don't do any of that stuff. If the interview is with one person it's apparent always that it's them speaking.

By the way, LET YOUR EGO AS A JOURNALIST STAND

OFF-STAGE. You prompt your interviewee on behalf of the audience. You don't need: 'He then went on to grumble about . . .' just go ahead with the grumble. (See example write-up in Chapter 18.)

DON'T SHOW IT TO THEM

STUDENT PAUL   Would you ever show the subject what you've written?

DARRYL   No – never. If they insist, you can do one of two things: either say 'Yes,' then forget all about it; or read it to them over the phone with the understanding that they correct errors of fact – but not the style. I wouldn't go to an artist and say: 'I don't like the way you've drawn that.' They'd be outraged. The same thing applies; what I do is my creative work too.

CHAPTER 23

Magnum Opus

THIS IS the exercise to end all exercises – a Magnum Opus.

As much as an operation in interviewing and writing, this is also a multimeasure in analysing, making contacts, communicating, overcoming shyness, and not being afraid to ask for help from other writers.

1 *Find at least one other beginner journalist/writer.*

Two of the simplest methods are to join a Writers' Club or go on a course in journalism or creative writing.

If the club/class meets on a night where you have another regular appointment, try and change it. If the journey is difficult, well tough! Potential journalists have to be prepared to make more effort than the ordinary person-in-the-street or they'll never become journalists.

A third method is to form your own Writers' Club – I tell you how in Chapter 9.

When you've got other writers to refer to, this is your (and their) scenario.

2 *Write a 500 to 1,000 word profile on one person or news feature that involves interviewing a number of people.*

If it's a profile, find the most interesting person you can – someone with an unusual job or hobby. For a news feature, they will have to have achieved/or be aiming at something newsworthy. If you can find a celebrity or an exceptional newsworthy person, then your objective will be to use this Magnum Opus exercise as a means towards getting it published in a magazine or your local newspaper.

Deadline MS to be in your hands **A** _____

Date actually received _____

NAME of Writer _____

Address _____

_____

Phone [day] _____ [eve/w'end] _____

Headline/Title _____ MARKET _____

Monitor, this Writer will send you their MS. At the meeting on **B** _____ (date) please give a report on the points an EDITOR will look for. Award marks on a scale of 0 to 10 (0 is low, and 10 is high). Then total them and write a brief critique to read to the group.

	0	1	2	3	4	5	6	7	8	9	10	TOTAL
Received on deadline												
Market suitability												
Is ANGLE new?												
Good/bad opening?												
Good/bad ending?												
Plenty of quotes?												
Any clichés?												
Informative piece?												
Entertainingly written?												
Good SHORT sentences?												
Is it written to length?												
Tenses												
Grammar												
Punctuation												
Spelling												
Layout typed correctly?												

GRAND TOTAL

CRITIQUE:

3 _Agree a common deadline with the others in your group – perhaps two months from now – when you will deliver your finished, polished typescript (handwritten pieces not accepted)._

This is sacrosanct. Take photocopies for every group member of the form above (you may like to enlarge it) and enter the deadline top right 'A'. Fill in ONLY your name, address and phone numbers in the spaces provided. Each person has a form and fills in their own personal details.

Agree a date two weeks after the deadline, to be entered in space 'B'. This will be a meeting of the whole group.

.4 *Post/give your finished Magnum Opus to a Monitor, i.e. one of the people in your group, by deadline, before if possible.*

The best way to chose a monitor is to write the names of everyone in the group on separate pieces of paper, fold them in four and put them in a hat. Everyone then 'lucky dips' for their own monitor.

Treat your monitor with serious respect – as you would an editor. Your typescript MUST be received on the deadline specified (NB: received, not put in the post). There are only two possible marks for the first item 'Received on deadline': 0 or 10.

The title/headline and the market aimed at should be on the first page of the Magnum Opus so the monitor can enter these details on the form when s/he receives the work.

5 *The monitor analyses the write-up according to the 16 items listed, and gives marks. S/he then totals them and writes a brief critique to read to the group.*

This way everyone gets an opportunity to interview, to write, and to analyse a piece of work other than their own.

I give this exercise to my students – many of whom have said it helped them a great deal. If you do find it useful, and if you have any successes, do write and let me know – I'd love to hear about them.

BUT SORRY, I CAN'T OFFER TO CRITICISE WORK, so please don't send me your unpublished pieces.

Good luck with your interviewing.

Index

Piatkus Books

If you enjoyed this book, you may be interested in reading other books on writing and journalism published by Piatkus.

Journalism for Beginners: How to get into print and get paid for it   Joan Clayton

How to Make Money from Freelance Writing   Andrew Crofts

1000 Markets for Freelance Writers: An A–Z guide to general and specialist magazines and journals   Robert Palmer

Writing Your Life Story   Nancy Smith

The Fiction Writer's Handbook   Nancy Smith

An Author's Handbook   David Bolt

For a free brochure with further information on our complete range of titles, please write to:

> **Piatkus Books**
> Freepost 7 (WD 4505)
> London
> W1E 4EZ

PIATKUS

Journalism for Beginners
Joan Clayton

Journalism for Beginners is the essential guide for everyone who wants to write features and earn money from them. It shows you how to:

● come up with ideas that sell

● develop a punchy style

● write hard-hitting news reports

● give editors what they want

● handle productive interviews

● write profiles and reviews

● get into radio journalism

Journalism for Beginners tells you everything you need to know. It is packed with essential advice, exercises to build your skills and confidence, inside information and invaluable hints and tips. *Journalism for Beginners* will ensure you get into print *and* get paid for it.

Joan Clayton is a journalist and editor. The excellent journalism courses she runs are renowned for getting students into print before the end of their course.